The Boy Who Lost His Birthday

A Memoir of Loss, Survival, and Triumph

Laszlo Berkowits with Robert W. Kenny

Edited by Jody I. Franklin

Hamilton Books

A member of
The Rowman & Littlefield Publishing Group
Lanham • Boulder • New York • Toronto • Plymouth, UK

Hamilton Books
4501 Forbes Boulevard
Suite 200
Lanham, Maryland 20706
Hamilton Books Acquisitions Department (301) 459-3366

Estover Road
Plymouth PL6 7PY
United Kingdom

Library of Congress Control Number: 2008926964
ISBN-13: 978-0-7618-4065-7 (clothbound : alk. paper)
ISBN-10: 0-7618-4065-6 (clothbound : alk. paper)
ISBN-13: 978-0-7618-4066-4 (paperback : alk. paper)
ISBN-10: 0-7618-4066-4 (paperback : alk. paper)
eISBN-13: 978-0-7618-4181-4
eISBN-10: 0-7618-4181-4

My Parents
Zsanett and Herman Berkovits

My Siblings
Ilona, Iren (Chanah), Sandor and Katalin

Judy
My soulmate

My Children
Julie Berkowits Poggioli and her husband Peter
Deborah Berkowits Litwak and her husband Alan

My Grandchildren
Zoe and Samuel Poggioli
Hannah, Naomi and Yael Litwak

Adas Israel Congregation
Derecske, Hungary 1850–1944

But take utmost care and watch yourselves scrupulously, so that you do not forget the things that you saw with your own eyes and so that they do not fade from your mind as long as you live. And make them known to your children and your children's children.

Deuteronomy 4:9

Contents

*For Alec
Rabbi Laylo Borkaul*

Preface

In 2003, I visited my childhood home of Derecske, Hungary. Waiting for me in the mayor's office was a book that he had personally inscribed to me, *The History of Derecske and Its People* by a Hungarian historian Gazdag Istvan. When I read the book upon my return home, I was shocked to discover that the facts about the deportation of Derecske's Jews to Auschwitz-Birkenau were absent from the narrative. According to this published history, Derecske's Jews were taken from the town's marketplace to NagyVarad, the region's primary ghetto. There the story ends.

No mention of their deportation to Auschwitz-Birkenau. No mention of their mass murder.

How could that be?

I am a survivor of the Nazi concentration camps in Poland and Germany. During World War II, I was in German hands from July 8, 1944 to May 2, 1945 and was held in five different concentration camps: Auschwitz-Birkenau, Braunschweig, Watenstedt, Ravensbruck, and Wobbelin. As a survivor, I feel a duty to history to record my eyewitness account of the near-annihilation of Hungarian Jewry.

I also wish to preserve the sacred memories of the spirited community in which I spent the first fourteen years of my life, a community and a style of life that has been obliterated as though it had never been. I have a strong sense of obligation to my childhood community to preserve a portrait of a once vibrant, colorful, God-fearing, God-loving community. I cannot erect a monument to Derecske but I can write this tribute to preserve and honor its memory.

As a child, I believed that my Jewish community had existed for centuries. I was shocked to learn, as I did only recently, that the Jewish community of Derecske in which I grew up was on the Hungarian map for fewer than a hundred years, from 1852 to 1944. While the entire history of the Derecske Jewish community spanned less than a century, it developed a vigorous, if self-contained, life, a vibrant life that was comfortable and decent for most people most of the time.

Derecske, in northeastern Hungary near the Romanian border, was a dusty farm town of about 11,000 people, of whom 800 or so were Jewish. They were hardworking people, observant Jews whose lives were ruled by the religious calendar. Holidays—truly holy days, serious and fun-filled—that came and went with the seasons, gave the year its variety and color. Passover, the most important of the spring holidays, was especially festive, with its joyous celebration of the Jewish liberation from Egyptian slavery and the birth of the Jewish people into freedom. Passover's theme of liberation has become the inspiration for many of the oppressed people of the earth. "Let my people go" became the mantra of the enslaved. Growing up, I had no inkling that my community would again have to live through slavery to gain freedom. Yet, only a few of us survived to witness the end of World War II.

Acknowledgments

I wish to acknowledge the encouragement and assistance of the following people:

Bob Kenney, who first encouraged me to record my memories of my experiences during WWII, has been an indispensable mentor for me. Without him, this book would never have been undertaken or completed.

My deep appreciation goes to Sam and Susan Simon, Marshall Berman and Karen Kaplan, Barbara and Cal Klausner for their many years of friendship and their dedication to the publication of this book.

I thank Devra Massey for her friendship and encouragement.

I thank my colleagues Rabbi Richard Sternberger and Rabbi Amy Schwartzman for their encouragement.

I am deeply grateful to my secretary Anne Duncan for always being there when I need her.

Finally, I thank Jody Franklin for her excellent professional work in editing this memoir. I am grateful for her creative spirit and insightful editing of the manuscript.

Introduction

Many memoirs of the Holocaust have been published; they number easily in the hundreds. The smallest sampling of them will suggest the unique horror of that most depraved episode of human experience. At the same time, even taken all together they cannot encompass the scale of its horror. Each survivor has carried individual and particular memories that could illuminate another dark corner that could contribute something more to a universal understanding of what will always stand as a central event of the twentieth century.

With the liberation of the death camps now more than half a century in the past, time is now the enemy of history. It becomes easier and easier to live in ignorance of events that most of the world's population is too young to remember. In that ignorance, the anti-historians can busily minimize or even deny the reality of tragedy. Indeed, the tragedy was so vast, so staggering, that we would like to believe it could not have happened; our unwillingness to look horror in the face gives those who deny history a specious kind of plausibility. Each day the number of people who really know what happened is diminished; the survivors are aging rapidly. A thirty-year-old man captured on the streets in Budapest in the summer of 1944 would now have reached the age of ninety-three. Among even the most vigorous, memories fade and limbs falter. Inevitably, it is now the case that only those who were young when taken are likely to be still living. If they were taken when quite young, it was overwhelmingly likely that they were put to death almost at once; small children had little or no potential value as slave labor. So the great majority of those who now survive were teenagers when they fell into Nazi hands—old enough and strong enough to be seen as having labor value but young enough to reasonably have lived another sixty-odd years. The perspective of teenagers may differ in important ways from that of their elders: different things may attract their notice; different stratagems might be employed for survival. Still, it is upon the sharpness of their memories that we must rely.

There is a basic sense in which the experience of every survivor is alike. Every one endured humiliation, degradation, and deprivation for months that had to seem endless. Every one had to become accustomed not only to immediate misery and total helplessness but to the possibility, even the expectation, of death today, tomorrow, or the day after. Every one experienced the loss of family, of cultural context, of meaningful personal history. Every one survived because of some combination of inner strength, determination, and sheer luck. Every story has some episode in which the workings of chance meant the difference between life and death: if I had turned right instead of left at that corner, if I had answered yes instead of no to that question, if I had chosen to stand in that line rather than this one, I would not be here.

But if one story is like another in outline, every one is unique in its details, and it is the details that make their contribution to the composite history. So the story of Laszlo Berkowits, like the stories of every other survivor, is unique and important. He was brought up in a poor family in a town far from the centers of power and information, part of a tightly knit Orthodox community, a community that was to a remarkable degree internally focused and oblivious to the political maelstrom that was gathering elsewhere. That his family was poor meant that he did not travel, read newspapers, or listen to a radio. His community was concerned first of all with the daily routines of living within the rules of the Orthodox life. A boy growing up in that community lived in a cocoon; Laszlo himself never entered the house of a non-Jew and never played with a Gentile child. His world was the world of the schoolroom and the synagogue. The Jews of the town were by no means as isolated as those in the ghettoes further to the east; they had daily contact through their work with the non-Jewish population, but the town as a whole had very little direct connection with the chaos outside Hungarian borders. Nobody had much knowledge of the politics that would determine Hungary's destiny.

In the spring of 1943, he went to Budapest to join his father, who had taken work in the Jewish cemetery; the rest of the family was left behind. At that moment, it was financial exigency rather than religious persecution that was driving them. His father worked for the registrar of graves and Laszlo in the greenhouses. Together they were able to send money home for the support of his mother and younger siblings. And at first, he saw a vast world of possibility and opportunity in a sophisticated and highly cultured city.

The circumstances of Hungary's Jews by 1944 have a special kind of poignancy. Earlier in the war, they had hoped to retain a degree of protection from the fact that Hungary was technically not an occupied territory but a German ally. Its government was in the hands of Hungarians, at least some members of which at some times had recognized the Jews as contributing citizens. The Kallay government in particular, in power from March 1942 to March 1944, the time during which the destruction of so much of European Jewry had occurred, had consistently resisted German efforts to apply their "Final Solution" to Hungary. Jews had wider and more comprehensive rights than in many parts of Europe, particularly in the East. They could and often did own real estate; they were conspicuous in academic and medical professions. Those rights had been whittled away, beginning as early as 1938, when legislation defining "a Jew" was passed—even before Germany was putting pressure on the Hungarian government. Later laws broadened that definition and placed limits on Jewish participation in many professions, particularly those with higher social standing. But the fact that the middle class was comprised almost entirely of Jews meant that barring Jews from most kinds of trade and manufacturing would be a national economic catastrophe. Even the most hostile of the Hungarian governments had to recognize that its war effort would be crippled by closing down Jewish factories and businesses. Jewish leadership, however reluctantly, accepted the restrictions, each time believing—or hoping—that acquiescence in one set of restrictions would satisfy their persecutors, sometimes simply hoping that they could hold off more drastic steps until help came from the outside. It would not be too difficult to surmise the likely mindset of the Jewish leadership in Budapest. Almost certainly they believed help would come if they had held out a little longer. They had some knowledge, not widely shared, of what had happened to Jews in Germany and the conquered lands, but they clung to the belief that Hungary would be different. And in the spring and early summer of 1944, it might have seemed that they were right, that the war would be over before Hungary's Jews would be destroyed. Russian armies were advancing relentlessly across the wide Eastern Front; Americans and British were pushing north through Italy, and on June 6th, enormous Allied forces landed in Normandy. German resources were strained to the breaking point. A rational German government might have found it prudent to forget about Hungary's Jews and focus its efforts on survival or negotiation. But Hitler's regime was anything but rational. It was, however, consistent. The goal of exterminating Jewry overrode all considerations of strategy, practicality, or common sense. Even if the regime was doomed, it was unwavering in its determination that the last remnants of Europe's Jews should be doomed as well.

On March 19, 1944, the Germans occupied Budapest. The Kallay government had been toppled and replaced by German puppets. Adolf Eichmann came in person to supervise this last operation against Europe's Jews. On March 31, he summoned the leadership of the Budapest Jewish communities to a meeting where they were ordered to create a *Judenrat* that would channel

German orders to the people, to publish a newspaper that would carry German instructions, to create new labor battalions, and produce requisitioned materials and supplies. As he had in parallel circumstances, he said that the Jews had nothing to fear if they cooperated, that they would not be molested, and that when the war was over everything would return to normal. Still hoping that their experience would be different from that of all the other Jews of occupied Europe, the Budapest leaders eagerly agreed, and the *Judenrat* became the tool of German policy. Within days, the wearing of yellow stars was ordered, travel was prohibited, and thousands of Jewish businesses were shut down. Several thousand who tried to move about the city without permission were arrested. In April the country was divided into zones and the deportations began, beginning with the small towns; Budapest would be last. Once begun, the deportation moved with lightning speed; in one ten-day period, almost 140,000 Jews were sent by train from Hungarian towns to Auschwitz. By early May, contact with towns like Derecske was lost; their Jewish communities were gone forever.

For a few brief months that spring in Budapest, in the face of increasing Nazi presence and mounting persecution, Laszlo was able to relish a taste of the freedoms and the culture of one of Europe's most sophisticated cities. Separated from the strict Orthodox environment, he began to move away from its rules and restrictions, to the dismay of his father. That movement would eventually lead him to embrace the Reform Jewish movement. But as an adolescent, he had no real grasp of the perils of the situation in which he lived. He watched newsreels in the movie houses and read newspapers, but what they offered was only what had been passed by the censors. The anti-Jewish restrictions he tried, with the careless bravado of a teenager, to evade. But in early June, just after D-Day, life suddenly changed. Arrested in a cemetery, he then spent almost a year in concentration camps and labor camps, struggling, as everybody did, to survive another day. Compared to some stories, his seems superficially less dramatic: he was never tortured, he did not become a sex slave or a medical experiment, he had no role in the deaths of other prisoners or German guards, he made no heroic or foolhardy attempts at escape. He endured and kept on enduring. In that respect, his story is probably typical of most survivors: they survived in part because they attracted no special notice. Living in the shadows was at least staying alive. It took a measure of luck and a great deal of what might be called animal intelligence— "street smarts" in modern parlance—to blend successfully into the gray mass of captives for months on end. He was aided, much more than he probably knew at the time, by the fact of having lived with privation, and by the fortuitous possession of a prayer book, which focused his mind. And which may have pointed him, subconsciously, toward his later career.

Taken in June of 1944 and liberated the following May, his ordeal was far shorter than those experienced by Jews of Poland, Germany, and other parts of Europe. But it is representative of Hungarian Jewry, which had felt protected and insulated through much of the war. The way of life for Hungarian Jews who lived in ignorance—or perhaps, in part, denial—of what was happening elsewhere is of great interest to both historians and the interested public. This teenage boy's and his father's perceptions of the wider world aid our present understanding of why events unfolded in Hungary as they did.

The inner strength required of survivors often marked them for success in later life. In the case of Laszlo Berkowits, known as Larry to his friends and congregants, he became a religious leader of distinction. After his rabbinical training, he accepted a position with a fledgling Reform congregation in the Virginia suburbs of Washington, D.C. At that time it had a bare handful of members, no building, and little money. Focusing on a religious service that was warm and welcoming and that made use of his magnificent cantorial voice, he built what has grown to be the biggest congregation in the Commonwealth of Virginia. Thirty years later, Temple Rodef Shalom has to be counted one of the most successful Reform synagogues in the country. It is a proud legacy.

For Rabbi Berkowits, preparing this memoir became an imperative after a visit to the sites of his youth and imprisonment. After he had turned over his rabbinical pulpit to an able successor, he took a group of his congregants on a trip to Eastern Europe. They went to Budapest, Prague, and Auschwitz. He was able to locate where his barracks had stood and to stand on the field where the final selection had taken place. It was for all of them a time of great emotional significance; most of them had relatives, close or distant, who had died at Auschwitz. But one aspect of the trip was especially disturbing: everywhere they went, they were met with silence about the past. During a separate trip to Derecske, where he had grown up, it was as though there had never been a Jewish community; nobody talked about it or apparently even remembered. Around Auschwitz, it seemed that the past had been papered over; there were even few and minimalist guideposts to the site. So he returned with the conviction that it was a responsibility, a duty to those who never left Auschwitz, to add his story to those of the other survivors, so that the record of those horrors could be a little more complete.

Robert W. Kenny
Professor Emeritus
The George Washington University
June 2008
Stony Brook, New York

Chapter One

My World

As a boy, my entire world was the town of Derecske, a charmed world replete with natural physical beauty, close family relationships, and robust Jewish tradition. More than a village, but less than a city, Derecske was a pastoral town on the rich agricultural plains of northeastern Hungary. My childhood was joyously grounded in my family and my religious faith. My family was poor but, like most of the families I knew at the time, was rich in warmth, love and a sense of purpose.

In the 1930s, as it had been for generations, Derecske was surrounded by farms, orchards, and gardens. The town spread out from a crossroad where the north-south road, which led to Hungary's second largest city, Debrecen, in the north and the town of Berettyoujfalu in the south, met the east-west road, one going toward Romania in the east and the other leading west through central Hungary and, eventually, to Budapest. Other lanes and roads, stretching to outlying villages and farms, fed into the two main streets, dusty tracks in the summer and frozen ruts in the winter.

Derecske had two railroad stations, which was unusual for such a small town. The only paved road led to the main railroad station about a kilometer from the center of town. Even the sidewalk that led to the station was paved. The station had a busy freight and passenger service to Debrecen; some of the town's residents traveled to the city every day to work or study. For small town people in Eastern Europe, to have come from a town that had two railroad stations became a mark of status, something to brag about.

Derecske's important public buildings, such as the town hall, the high school, the courthouse, and the churches, were situated north of the main intersection. The principal stores and merchants—the hardware and dry goods shops, grocers, tailors, butchers, bakers, shoemakers and clothiers—were also in the north part of town. Some of the buildings along the main street were two stories, with the shops below and living quarters for the owners' families above. Smaller shops had living spaces in the rear, behind bolts of cloth or farm implements, candles and kerosene lamps.

For centuries, the town and the lands around it belonged to the Esterhazy family, one of the richest and most powerful noble families in Central Europe. The Esterhazys had been statesmen, patrons of art and music, builders of castles, advisors to emperors and kings. (The family's name had been marred by one of its members who, after having resettled in France, was found guilty of forging documents that convicted Captain Alfred Dreyfus of treason.) By the time I was born, the Esterhazy presence had disappeared, but some of the family's land was still held in great estates where the farmers worked as tenants. The estates were, of course, broken up during the Communist years, but the farmers followed the same pattern of life that they led in the 1930s and 1940s, tending their crops and bringing them to market.

Before 1850, only a tiny handful of Jewish families who had been given special permits by the Esterhazy family had lived in Derecske. Without the special permits, Jews were prohibited from living there. Their number gradually grew, either because the Esterhazy lords lifted restrictions on Jewish settlement as part of a conscious strategy for economic development or simply because the authorities hadn't paid attention. Jewish families began to drift in, arriving mostly from Poland and the Carpathian Mountains in Romania.

My town's landscape was dominated, as was true in most European towns, by its largest church. Baroque in style, the church was painted bright yellow on the lower level, pale yellow on the top, with white trim all around; the tall steeple was painted copper. Unlike most of Hungary whose dominant religion was Catholic, the big church in Derecske was Protestant. Its tall tower, with a clock on each of its four sides, could be seen from all over town. Though I learned to tell time from those clocks, I never ventured inside the church's doors. The church, like the city of Debrecen, belonged to a world of which I had no part. Simply being physically close to the church made me vaguely uneasy and, walking past it, on my way to the railroad station or to visit someone on the other side of town, I would cross the street to avoid it. I didn't want to come too near its front doors. On some unspoken, visceral level, I believed that to cross the street was a symbolic act of spiritual separation from all that the church and its members represented and, in some unacknowledged emotional way, addressed the alienation that I, as a Jew, felt from their world.

Derecske was comprised of about 11,000 people, of which only 800—125 families—were Jews. While everyone in the town shared the same language, its residents did not share the same culture. We were of totally different worlds, living side by side, a separation that felt natural to me at the time.

Included in my town's other world was a small Catholic church and a tiny Nazarine chapel. Only a few doors away from the chapel was the synagogue my family attended. While the churches exist today exactly as they were then, the synagogue is gone and a health clinic has been built in its spot. The synagogue is not missed: there are no longer any Jews in Derecske.

Derecske's buildings were modest. Most houses were one story and made of what Americans call adobe, mud bricks plastered over and whitewashed or painted. The houses were primarily roofed with thatch, though an occasional roof was made of tile. Few people grew flowers or landscaped their small yards; hardworking farmers and shopkeepers didn't have the time or interest and our yard was no different. Nonetheless, acacia trees, laden with fragrant blossoms in the spring, filled the streets for weeks with their fragrant sweet aroma. No one had indoor plumbing and only a few of the wealthier houses had electricity; my house had neither. As a result, we were quite isolated: no electricity meant no radios—which meant that my family and I, and most of our community, knew little of what was going on in the rest of the world.

Derecske's dreariness didn't bother me: it was my home. While I desired more for myself, I was attached to my hometown, my family and relatives and was in no way eager to leave. I played with friends for hours upon hours, soccer and other outdoor games of our own imagination. Often, I visited relatives who lived only a short walk away.

Derecske is twenty or so kilometers south of Debrecen, a great commercial center and home to an historic university. Though Debrecen was easily reachable by road or rail, I never went there as a child; not even once. For me, Debrecen might as well have been on another planet. I envied those who were able to go to school there; I knew it was a place with style and sophistication and, while I loved my home, I also longed to be part of that world.

While young, I had an idea that I would move from Derecske some day despite the fact that no one I knew traveled much. Travel was limited not by the means of transportation—trains and wagons could connect us with the rest of the world—but by work. Farmers were tied to their crops and their livestock, and shop owners to their shops. I had been right that I would leave Derecske, but in no way did I envision how my journey away from Derecske would begin.

Of my town's 125 Jewish families, some were businessmen, large and small; some were craftsmen and others peddlers. Five men owned land, and fourteen families with no means of support received public charity. Except for a co-op and one large grocery store, Jews were the merchants of Derecske. Some stores were like little factories, cottage industries. Craftsmen, such as the Farkas family, with five to ten shoemakers, made boots and shoes, for example, in the back rooms of their shop and displayed their samples in a showroom in front. Using sheets of tanned leather, they custom-made tall, elegant boots, rather like English riding boots. Christian peasant boys aspired to own a pair to wear on Sundays, polished and shined to a mirror-like gloss. I hoped for a pair myself but knew I could never afford one. One neighbor dealt in leather goods to supply the shoemakers. He also sold shoe parts—soles or uppers, brown or black, usually calfskin—to be sized by the shoemaker. The rich smell of leather still exerts a powerful pull on my memories of that time of my life.

My godfather, Jozsef Weiss, owned one of the biggest stores in town. I don't know why my parents asked Weiss to be my godfather or why he accepted, though it certainly was a great honor to have him serve that role. There was no blood relationship and he was not a close social friend. Perhaps my parents asked him with the hope that he would be a kind benefactor—which he was. After the war, when he learned that I had survived, he continued to maintain an interest in me.

Weiss owned a clothing shop with a few tailors who worked from their homes. In order for a farmer to buy a suit, often he would have to sell his crops, a horse or a cow. Once the proud owner of a new suit, he would wear it for years and years, decades even. Since not many people bought such suits, they often hung in the shop windows a long time before they sold. Overcoats, made of heavy wool from Czechoslovakia or England, lasted even longer than a suit; a man might have only two in a lifetime. When I was twelve years old, I worked occasionally after school in my godfather's shop, dusting the merchandise. While my godfather sold new goods, another tailor, Abraham, specialized in re-making old suits—the fabric would be turned inside out and re-fashioned, usually for someone, perhaps a son, who needed a smaller size. Derecske did not ship goods out to the rest of Hungary or the world; the products made in these little shops were intended for local consumption.

Several stores served the needs of local farmers—hardware stores that sold tools and farm implements, merchants who bought and sold hay and grain. Down the street from the main marketplace was my uncle Aron Jakab's house; he was a hay merchant who had giant haystacks in his back yard. He bought hay in the summer and sold it in the winter when the farmers' stock ran low. The hay had to be stacked carefully so that the heat that would accumulate inside would not start a fire; constantly aware of the danger of a potential fire, he would push sticks into the stacks to test the temperature.

Solomon Rubin, the grain merchant and one of the wealthiest men in town, lived across the street from my uncle. Solomon also had a residence in Budapest—the first man I knew to outgrow our town. Like everybody else, his Derecske business and home were combined in one location, situated on a big corner lot on Main Street, with a wooden granary in back. Farmers would bring wheat or corn to his house. A crew of men, which included my father every once in a while, carried the sacks of grain from the wagons to the big scale, weighed it, and then carried the grain to the bins where they would dump it. They were paid according to how much they carried; a day's wages might be the equivalent of half a dollar or a dollar—not much for such heavy work.

Solomon's brother Lajos Rubin, a successful merchant in firewood and coal, was the father of my close friend Arthur. Arthur and I grew up together. We attended school together from the age of four and to this day he is my most precious friend.

I recall one merchant in particular who owned a large grocery store on one corner of the main intersection across from the outdoor farmer's market. His annual displays of Christmas delicacies—chocolates, figs, oranges—attracted admiring glances from all children. A dozen or so Jewish grocers were scattered around town, four or five of them on Main Street. The grocery stores were my favorite shops; whenever I had pocket money, I would go to the grocery for rock candy that I would suck on for hours to make it last as long as possible.

Derecske contained two Jewish-owned inns—they would be considered bars in today's America—where the local men gathered to drink and sing, often becoming drunk, boisterous, and bad-tempered. Loud quarrels and fights were common. Since Jewish men of that time and place mostly confined their drinking to sacramental wine, owning a bar might seem a curious occupation, but an economic niche had to be filled. Social drinking was not part of my family's lifestyle and none of the Jews in Derecske patronized the bars.

Finally, our town had doctors as well. The town's most beloved doctor was Jewish, Dr. Arthur Berger, and his clientele crossed class and religion. Once a year, he would ride to our school on his bike and give us a physical exam—which didn't involve much beyond looking down our throats. He died very young—he caught pneumonia after riding on his bike in a cold rain to visit a sick person on an outlying farm. His funeral was a major social event, with a great outpouring of affection.

Most farmers had wood-fired ovens at home, conical constructions of plastered clay located in the entryway of the farmhouse, but Jewish families did not. They made bread dough at home and carried it in wicker baskets to the baker. Our town had two Jewish bakers, Lustig and Moskowitz. Both bakeries had wood-burning ovens. Lustig's shop was across the street from my Hebrew school and the aroma of baking rye bread drifted out, capturing the attention of the boys and sharpening their hunger as they pored over their school books inside or played outside during recess. I would drop off our family's dough in the morning on the way to school and pick it up on the way home. Sometimes I would use a wheelbarrow to carry three unbaked loaves, two large and one small, to the baker on my way to school. I would pick up the small one when I went home for lunch and my father would pick up the other loaves when he came home in the evening. At lunch, we enjoyed the bread still warm from the oven, with soup. It was wonderful rye bread in a crispy crust, the best bread in the world.

The bakers also cooked the traditional Sabbath meal for Jews across Hungary—a dish called *cholent*, made with kidney beans and perhaps a piece of meat, covered with *kugel*, a dish made of flour and *schmaltz* (rendered or melted chicken fat), pepper, salt, and paprika. As was true throughout Eastern Europe, beans were a mainstay of our diet, incorporated in some manner into our favorite dishes. My mother prepared the cholent and kugel at home in a big clay pot. She sealed the pot with brown wrapping paper and wrote *Berkowits* on top. On our way to synagogue late Friday afternoon, we would drop it off at the bakery. The dish would cook all night in the oven. Cooking on the Sabbath was not allowed, but this was permissible in Jewish law because the oven had already been heated before sunset. Saturday morning, when the morning service was over, we would go to the bakery and pick up the cholent. It was a wonderful, unbroken tradition followed in both summer and winter.

My family was close-knit. My father, Herman, was a silent man, not prone to conversation. He was the disciplinarian in our home, as in most Hungarian families, and he could be tough. He was a man of tremendous integrity and devotion, deeply pious, with an absolute, unwavering commitment to Orthodox Judaism. The life of faith meant everything to him.

My father had been trained as a carpenter or cabinetmaker, but for a reason unknown to me, he did not practice that trade. He patch-worked a livelihood in bits and pieces. He performed odd jobs about town, sometimes working for one neighbor, sometimes another. If a fair took place, he might try to sell a hodgepodge of goods. I think he was reconciled to the idea that he would always be poor, but he did not blame himself because so many of our neighbors were poor as well. In order to help make ends meet, sometimes my mother would go to peasant homes on some of the larger estates to sell candles, soap, and flypaper. I never had the chance to talk to him about how he felt about not being able to provide better for his family.

In contrast to my father, my mother, Zsanett—Zisele in Yiddish, meaning "sweet one"—was pure love. She was an unbelievable homemaker. How she could do everything that she did under such basic circumstances—cook, clean, raise her children, sew—is a wonder to me to this day.

I had three sisters and one brother: blonde, blue-eyed and quiet Ilona, six years older; spirited and daring Iren with brown hair and hazel eyes, two years older; my cute youngest sister, Kato, four years younger; and finally my quiet brother Sandor, six years younger.

My father's father, Mihaly Berkovits, managed a farm near the town of Berettyoujfalu; he lived there with his second wife, my step-grandmother. Our contact with them was intermittent; while the farm was only nine kilometers away, the trip by horse and buggy, on a single-lane country road was long. One summer, when I was eight, I spent two wonderful weeks with them, the closest thing I ever had to a summer vacation. My grandmother was a woman of few words, at least with me. But despite her silence, she must have liked me, because she made me a pair of long white cotton pants, rather like pajamas, the kind local farmers wore in the summer. My grandfather took me with him as he worked so I could see life on the farm of golden wheat, corn and potato fields. And cattle: I found the cattle and the lordly bull fascinating. I remember one occasion when a young farmhand had finished milking a cow; she dipped a cup into the large pail and gave me a drink of the warm, foamy fresh milk. One evening, we celebrated the birthday of the daughter of another tenant farmer. The girl and her family, like all the tenant farmers, lived in a small, white house of bare adobe; that evening the house rang with joyous folk singing. At night, I slept on a little cot in the corner of their room; as I fell asleep, I listened to the loud, unceasing tick-tock, tick-tock of their clock.

I was lucky to have had a host of second cousins, the children of my mother's first cousins, who also lived in Derecske. Having an extended family—colorful and boisterous, but who don't always get along—was a precious gift. It seemed that at least one half wasn't talking to the other half because of some quarrel or other. My relatives were very sensitive about status, easily insulted when they felt they had been overlooked. They all, including my mother, thought they were better than the others and were continually trying to establish a proper pecking order. On Yom Kippur, they asked forgiveness of each other because they couldn't go to the synagogue without talking to each other. But the dynamic would start over with the New Year.

I felt close to the Aron family. From the age of nine, I spent more and more time in their home. They were wealthy; they lived in a big house and had horses, which I loved. The family had six sons, all of whom became natural businessmen, turning straw into gold; they could sell anything, from tree leaves to animal skins, for a profit.

They also had a daughter, Alizka who was a year younger than I. For years she was my special playmate: we were together constantly, happy as larks, until I was about twelve when her mother, my Aunt Serena, must have told her she was too old to play with boys. I was sad when Alizka pulled away from me; I was so naïve that it was years before I understood why we had been separated. This was the first of many painful points of departure from my childhood, though this experience doesn't compare with those to come later.

I was closest to the youngest son in the Aron family, Shaiko, and we were very good friends. We were like Tom Sawyer and Huck Finn. Shaiko and I would spend hours playing in an orchard his father owned, causing trouble among the watermelons and other fruit. He was footloose, always ready for adventure, including playing hooky from religious school. Once I left school early, pretending to go to the outhouse, and met him in the school yard. He had a bicycle, a rare item among us; we rode double to his house, hitched up the horses to the wagon and drove to the next town, Berettyoujfalu, to buy hay. We loaded it on the wagon and returned home at nightfall. It was a great adventure that I paid for later that night at home; my father punished me because I had missed the evening service at synagogue, but the adventure was worth the price.

Later, Shaiko was drafted into the labor force and spent the war in forced labor camps, escaping the crueler fate of the concentration camps. When I was a student in Sweden after the war, I was relieved to learn from my sister Ilona that Alizka and Shaiko had survived the war and emigrated to Israel. We were all tearfully reunited there twenty years later.

Our town's Jewish students attended a secular school and a religious school that were housed in two separate rooms in the same building. The secular schoolroom was presided over by Geiger Bertha, a woman selected by the community but paid by the state. She had a gymnasium education and considered herself an intellectual. She lived apart from the community; I remember going to her home and feeling awed by the richness of the furniture and carpets. She taught several grades in a single classroom: while she gave the third grade a writing assignment, she would lecture the others about history or geography. To this day, I am one of many of her former students who still remember her fondly.

Severe and meticulous in manner, Geiger Bertha was very strict. If you were late to school in the morning, she would hit your hand with a cane. I was afraid of being late so I would often go to school without having eaten breakfast. My mother hated that I didn't eat and would come to school after I had arrived and settled into my seat. She would stand outside the window with my breakfast in her hand till I saw her. Eventually Geiger Bertha caught on and would announce in front of the entire school, "Berkowits! Your breakfast is here!"

The curriculum was truly basic—reading, writing, arithmetic, Hungarian history, geography, and a daily set of exercises, called gymnastics. The history was traditional: kings and battles. While I knew that Hungarian King Stephen converted to Christianity in the year 1000, I learned nothing of contemporary events. Still, our educations served most of us well enough; some of Geiger Bertha's students went on to gymnasium and university, and all became solid, decent people. She perished at Auschwitz.

Our school did not include organized sports, but outside of school we improvised games the best we could. Soccer was already popular throughout Europe and we were determined to play; no one had a soccer ball so we made do with an old tennis ball. Other games were less organized, such as pitching pennies against a wall. If we didn't have pennies, we pitched buttons we had cut off our jackets. In the winter after snowfalls, we made ice slides in the sloping courtyard of the school. When the ground thawed, usually a little after Purim, we would play with marbles. Other than the marbles, nobody had what could be called toys. I don't recall owning any toys that had been bought in a store. When I was small, my favorite toy was a rusty iron barrel hoop, which I would roll down the street to and from school.

At the end of the school year, an elaborate graduation ceremony was held in the courtyard under a tent so that the dignitaries of the congregation would be shielded from the sun. The students lined up in columns in the schoolyard and sang traditional Hungarian songs. Some of the words have stayed with me: *I would love to live in a gentle shadowy forest* . . . Speeches were given and every child brought flowers for the teacher. The graduation was a sad time for me because—rather than be pleased with my success—I was sad because the ceremony signaled the end of my childhood. I was twelve.

At the heart of town on Main Street was a plaza where, on Mondays and Fridays, the marketplace was held. Local farmers grew bountiful crops of wheat, corn, and onions that were sold at the market. (Derecske was famous for its onions; they were for Hungarians what Vidalia onions are for Americans.) Every Friday I went with my mother to the market to buy the Sabbath dinner. I loved to watch the wagons drawn by great oxen, laden with wheat, or corn, or oats in sacks. The farmers would sell their wares from their wagons or carts or stands they had set up. Most would set up where they had been before; there was a kind of informal agreement as to where each farmer should be. One woman maintained a permanent stand at the market, selling whatever was in season that might be eaten as snacks, such as apples, cherries, or sunflower seeds. Sunflower seeds were always popular; we chewed the seeds and spit out the shells on the street. I watched my mother examine the produce and bargain for the lowest price and helped her carry home the straw baskets laden with vegetables, potatoes, eggs and a live chicken.

Twice a year, the market turned into a huge fair for the whole district, bringing vendors from all over the region. The venders set up their stalls along a two-block promenade. At fair time, there was entertainment too, a traveling circus perhaps, or a foot-powered carrousel—some children would ride while others would push. The fair lasted for several days and created a holiday mood for the whole town. It was pure fun.

One kind of shop missing from Main Street was a dairy. Many farmers kept cows in a shed behind their houses and produced their own milk and cheese. Most Jews did not have cows; we bought milk directly from the farmer. There was no refrigeration, so milk was used fresh. It was boiled, though, except when it was used for making butter or cheese.

Every morning the shepherd's horn calling for the cows roused me from my night's sleep. I watched as the town's several hundred cows would come out of the side streets and merge into a moving mass on the wider road, whipping up a cloud of dust, heading to graze on the town's common pastures. At dusk, the cows would be brought home again, each one peeling off from the herd at the street leading to its home, turning right, turning left. The cows never got lost.

Chapter Two

Our Jewish Community

Derecske's organized Jewish community began in 1850 when a group of fifty Jews formed the town's first congregation. They erected a building the next year and five years later a full-time rabbi came from Nagy Szollos. He remained with the synagogue for over thirty years.

During my childhood in the 1930s, the center of Jewish life in Derecske was our synagogue and its rabbi, and I believe the seeds of my future profession as a rabbi were planted there. Our synagogue was comprised of separate buildings for summer and winter services, the *cheder* (the one room school) and *yeshiva*, a *mikvah* (a community ritual bath), a few houses, and a cemetery. The summer synagogue was made of light brown stucco with six tall windows on each side. The women's section was in the rear of the second floor and was unbearably hot. The winter synagogue was a simple building with a wooden floor and a cast-iron, coal-burning stove. The rabbi's house and the three school buildings (the cheder, the yeshiva, and the secular school) were clustered around a central courtyard.

Our strict Orthodox community of deep piety placed great emphasis on living according to the sacred laws of Judaism. The religious calendar governed the year: from Shabbat to Shabbat and holiday to holiday—the long summer days and interminable (to a child) fasting days, days commemorating the siege of Jerusalem and the destruction of the Temple. Our sexton, Reb Mandel, used to sing over and over a simple song of one sentence that captured the essence of the Messianic longing for redemption: *It won't be night forever; it will dawn someday.* Our Rosh Hashanah and Yom Kippur services remain etched in my memory for their beauty, simplicity, fervor, and musicality. Ours was a genuinely participatory worship; "everybody"—which at that time meant only men—took part in songs and prayers. As was the normal

Eastern European Orthodox practice, only men could take part in the daily services and the Sabbath evening service. Women attended only the holiday services. By the time I was ten, most nights after dinner I would walk with my father to the evening services.

Everyone knew how to pray and we were skillful in our worship to the point of art. Deep in our bones, we all understood the prayers and were familiar with the music. During the silent prayers, no one moved. The congregants knew what part of the service was the most important—useful information so you knew when you could go to the bathroom and when you needed to stay. My friends and I would play outside and listen through the open window so we would know when to go back in. *Sh'ma Yisrael Adonai Eloheinu Adonai Echad.* Except for my time in Auschwitz-Birkenau, never in my life have I been far from the world of Jewish worship.

Almost nobody missed Shabbat services, at least not in my family. Sometimes during the winter, though, we didn't go to the synagogue. One of our neighbors, Samuel Katz, was disabled and when the weather was bad he could not walk to the synagogue, so we would go to his house for the Shabbat morning worship. He was one of the innkeepers in town and had a big house with two levels, one for a residence and the other for the bar. My father liked to go there because it was a *mitzvah*, a good deed. I liked to go with him, because his wife was a wonderful baker; I remember the cheesecake and schnapps she served after the service.

Our religious system was a coherent, interrelated, and completely closed religious system, governed by a rabbi who, once elected, usually stayed for his entire working life. The rabbi, Zvi Hirsch Kohn, was a handsome, dignified man with a full beard, long black coat, and black hat. Our rabbi had supreme authority in all matters religious—and to us most matters had a religious dimension. He was the judge of the *Bet-Din*, the Jewish court, head of the yeshiva, and teacher for the adults. Our community highly respected and greatly loved him. While he did not participate in the general life of the community, he was consulted constantly on matters of tradition and practice.

Predictably, the community was not always of one mind on such issues. While everybody was Orthodox, some were more orthodox than others. Part of the community was *Hasidic* and, in some circumstances, separated itself from the other worshipers. The morning service for Pesach, for example, is divided into two parts, the Shacharit and Musaf. The Musaf is a service that in part replaces the animal sacrifices that were offered in the Temple in Jerusalem. One of the prayers, the *Kedushah*, or Sanctification, has several versions. Our rabbi followed one version; the Hasidim the other. So for the *Musaf* service, the few dozen Hasidic congregants would leave the summer synagogue and go to the *Bet Hamidrash*, the winter synagogue, and follow the other service. The Rabbi considered this to be an act of disrespect; it angered both him and his family. Once one of his sons walked up to the lectern in the winter synagogue and insulted the reader. These occasional frictions were seldom serious. Certainly the rabbi was considered a model of virtue and humility by virtually everyone. To me, he was closer to a concept of sainthood than anyone I knew.

The rabbi was assisted by several staff members: a *melamed* or teacher for the Hebrew school, a *shames* or sexton who looked after the buildings and a *shochet* who was the kosher slaughterer. The shochet also acted as a *mohel*, performing ritual circumcisions as Jewish male children entered the covenant of Abraham on the eighth day after birth.

One of the responsibilities of the shames was the care of the *mikvah*, the communal bath, heated in the winter but cool in summer. Since most houses did not have running water, the mikvah's functions were hygienic as well as religious, the only place where one could get a hot, soaking bath. Adult men went on Friday afternoons and before holidays and women went at other times. One hot summer afternoon, the rabbi's son, Hillel, and I broke into the mikvah to take a swim and cool off. That was a one-time adventure.

In addition to the men who were salaried, the community had a variety of people whose services were voluntary. An elected board of directors, comprised of well-regarded tradesmen, was responsible for the overall financial management and governance of the synagogue. A separate organization, the *Hevra Kadishah*, a Holy Society, had as its mission the care of the poor and hungry—to provide wood or coal for fuel and proper food for Passover—and to maintain the cemetery.

When someone died—most people died at home—the Hevra Kadishah arrived immediately. Their members would take care of the ritual bathing and dressing of the body and would arrange the funeral. Funerals were usually held within twenty-four hours of the death, in the yard of the person's home. The men of the Hevra Kadishah would build the casket in the yard, an hour before the funeral. One would bring a hammer, another a saw, and they would set to work. They would take the pieces of the casket inside, put it together, place the body in it, then carry it out again and place it on two sawhorses in the yard. The rabbi would lead the funeral service there. Afterward, the casket was taken on a horse-drawn wagon to the cemetery, where a solitary gravedigger dug the grave. I can still hear the Rabbi reciting in Hebrew: *It is a difficult burden for me to part with you.*

Every Friday, the rabbi, who was also the yeshiva teacher, would visit our school, a large, bare room with benches around the walls, a long table in the middle, a pot-bellied stove, and some bookcases in the corners with a few reference books. At precisely 11:30 A.M. the rabbi would test us on the weekly portion of Scripture. I watched as our teacher, Moshe Mendel Sternberg, ushered him in. In silence, the Rabbi would take a seat, carefully roll a cigarette, insert it in his silver holder, light it, take a first puff, exhale slowly, and say, "Let us begin." The students would sit at the long table, open Bibles in front of them, and wait to be called upon. As he smoked, he would pace back and forth in front of the table, stopping in front of this boy or that, and say, "Please read." Less than fully diligent students dreaded his visits. When the teacher left the room to fetch the rabbi, a few boys who didn't feel prepared would slip out. If Mr. Sternberg took the precaution of locking the door, desperate boys would exit through the window. Absences would not go unnoticed, but were not punished—the embarrassment of failure was punishment enough.

I remember one Friday before Hanukah when our exam was shorter than usual. The Rabbi pulled out of his pocket a handful of fillers, Hungarian pennies, and gave every student one. I ran out, through the yard, out the gate, to Klein's grocery store where I bought one penny's worth of rock candy. It was the best Hanukah present I ever received and years later I wrote a story about it that I called *The Rock Candy Hanukah*.

I was a good student, always ready to be called on; actually, most of the boys came to the Friday exam sessions reasonably well prepared; the teacher made sure of it. I normally knew my portion by Wednesday, so if a visitor came to town—a beggar or peddler—I would be chosen to show him around town. Jewish visitors were not uncommon, most often itinerant salesmen. They would come most frequently on Thursday or Friday and stay through the Sabbath. The house of the shames, which was owned by the synagogue, had an extra room where visitors stayed without charge. Our town had no hotels and welcoming strangers was a Jewish tradition.

Reb Mendel Sternberg was a firm disciplinarian and strict taskmaster. He had the charge of all the cheder, which took the boys from the age of four, as they began to learn Aleph and Bet. They were Reb Sternberg's responsibility until they were bar mitzvah at thirteen. Sarcasm was one of his pedagogical weapons, but it was a technique sometimes lost on his subjects. One day, frustrated over one boy's stubborn refusal to get his lesson right, he said, with a chuckle, "You know what? When you go home today, tell your father to go to Mr. Spitz, the tinsmith, and let him make a can big enough for your head; we'll put your head in there and send it to the British Museum, because I'm sure your head is one of a kind." None of us then knew what the British Museum was, so his point was rather blunted. I thought of Reb Mendel when I finally visited the British Museum in 1960; standing in front of the Elgin Marbles, I wished he could see me. He carried a long stick of cane and used it pretty freely; five raps across the hand or on the seat of the pants was the reward for inattention or rowdiness.

Some boys felt the cane regularly. I remember one day when an irate father came into the schoolroom, holding a big knife in his hand. "Reb Mendel," he said, "why do you torture my child every day? Here, do it once and for all — cut his throat and kill him." Our kind of discipline, of course, was normal in European schools before the war and, on the whole, we didn't resent it. Reb Mendel had a difficult job and the community respected him for it. My father never asked me if I liked the teacher — that was an inappropriate, irrelevant, question. But he often asked the teacher if I was doing well in school.

Boys began Hebrew education at the age of four learning their letters. By five or six, they began to study the prayer book and to attend morning and evening worship services with their fathers. By seven or eight, most were in control of the prayer book and began studying the Bible with its commentaries. At about nine, one studied the Mishnah and at ten the Talmud, the study of which could continue through life. We had to buy our own Bibles and prayer books. Reb Sternberg would inscribe them in flowing Hebrew calligraphy, 'This book belongs to . . .' adding one's Hebrew name, and then his own. After being bar mitzvah at thirteen, boys in the more Orthodox families were ready to go away to yeshiva where they would study Talmud and the Codes of Jewish Law until they reached the age of eighteen. Learning was highly valued; a learned Jew always commanded respect.

Next to the rabbi's house was the yeshiva, one long room with a Talmudic library attached. The rabbi taught fifteen or twenty students there, but not local boys. The custom was that, after bar mitzvah, one went somewhere else for further study. Some may have lived with the rabbi, but usually the boys stayed with local families. I believe poor families were paid a stipend to take in visiting students.

Boys had religious schooling through the entire year including the summer, every day except Saturday and the Jewish holidays. Girls received a minimal religious education, usually at home from their mothers. For the boys, schooling went from eight in the morning until six in the evening. In the mornings, we went to a secular school and after lunch, which we had at home, to Hebrew school.

I was jealous of my sisters who had freedom to play as they wished all summer long, but they were probably put to work at home. In the summer, we sometimes moved outdoors to the big courtyard and sat in the grass to study. Reeds with a hollow stem grew in the yard; sometimes, we could sneak time from our studies to cut sections of the reeds with our pocket-knives and make whistles or flutes. Some boys could play tunes on them.

My father loved religious studies and he was proud that I was studious. He was furious if I neglected cheder, but it didn't happen often. He shaped my consciousness of Jewish learning in a way that essentially shaped my life.

The purpose of Jewish education, of course, was the absorption and transmission of Judaism that was viewed as divinely ordained and unchanging. To enable individuals to participate competently in Jewish life, they needed to be knowledgeable about Jewish history, literature, prayer, and culture. Raising new generations who would be competent in religious life, familiar with the *mitzvot* and the commandments, knowing kosher and non-kosher, literate in worship, Talmud, and laws was tantamount in importance. Acquaintance with the foundations of Jewish law meant the ability to participate in Jewish life. Acceptance of the tradition was assumed, and violation of tradition, no matter how small, was a sin against the God of Israel. For the people who lived according to tradition in our town, life was deeply textured but isolated, ignorant of the currents of change that were sweeping through the world. When, for instance, our Rabbi heard that young Jews who were students at the university in Debrecen walked boldly outdoors without hats, he was deeply shocked. He took the occasion to complain from his pulpit, "What is this world coming to? Our young people walk down Main Street without hats on. They are destroying the foundations of Jewish life." He recognized a symptom of change that might lead anywhere.

From early times, I suspected that learning could be a way out of poverty. I knew I read Hebrew better than many of my classmates and suspected that being a good student could be liberating. From the time I was in the fourth grade, I saw older students going off to Debrecen for their studies and knew instinctively that they were entering a different world, one that I wanted for myself.

One day my cousin brought home from Debrecen an album of cantorial music by the great cantor Yoseleh Rosenblatt. I listened to the music over and over at my cousin's home on his family's hand cranked record player and learned to imitate it. I became very excited about Rosenblatt; the music struck a fundamental sympathetic chord in me. I realized, "I can do that," and I did. I had a beautiful voice, but it was more than that: I didn't just imitate his words—those were my words as well. I had grown up singing in the synagogue from the time I was eleven or twelve. Around the time of my bar mitzvah, the Rabbi needed boys to sing with him for the high holidays. Being chosen was a huge honor and he chose me. Our synagogue's services were so beautiful that people from nearby towns would come to worship with us. I saw music as a powerful vehicle of expression and I enjoyed people's reactions to my singing.

One of the great highlights of my early life was the celebration of my bar mitzvah in February 1941. It was a day of joy and pride for my entire family and the entire Jewish community during a time when the war was raging, especially on the Eastern front; the Germans had overrun nearly the whole of Europe, and the Hungarians were their somewhat willing allies. A bar mitzvah takes place near a boy's thirteenth birthday and marks the formal ending of his childhood and the beginning of the assumption of adult responsibilities for personal morality and conduct. My bar mitzvah was held in the winter synagogue, which had a big wood- and coal-burning stove in the middle of the room. Unfortunately, my mother and sisters could not attend because the winter synagogue was too small to have a women's section. I went off happily that morning with my father to take part in the service that made me, in the eyes of Jewish tradition, a full member of the community, able to be counted toward the *minyan* necessary for public worship.

I had been prepared by Reb Sternberg to recite in Hebrew a special reading from the Bible, from the Book of Kings, that dealt with the building of the First Temple in Jerusalem by King Solomon. I also sang the special blessings for the reading of the Torah and *Haftarah*, the supplemental Bible reading. I had looked forward to being called to the Torah because I knew I could sing my part better than anyone else. When I finished, I received many compliments from the worshippers.

Afterward, since our home was quite small, my Uncle Jakob and Aunt Serena hosted a reception for me at their house. Serena was a wonderful baker and had worked for several days, making cheese Danish and cinnamon and chocolate babkas. They also served schnapps and coffee, which contributed to the festive mood. I gave a brief speech concerning the purification of the vessels in the Temple at Jerusalem that the Rabbi's son, Leepeh, had helped me prepare. Though my remarks were of no great consequence, I believe they indicated some capacity for Jewish scholarship and the profession I would ultimately choose.

My mother cried a great deal during the reception. When I asked her why, she said, "If my mother were here, she would be so happy."

Understanding the emotional meaning behind the day's events, I replied, "If she were here, she would be crying too." The rabbi, friends, and members of my extended family, uncles and aunts and their children, were there. In those days, even well-to-do families had very modest receptions.

The day after the ceremony, I hastened to services thrilled to be considered a full adult in the eyes of Jewish law. When I arrived at the synagogue, a man asked me, "Boy, have you prayed yet?" When I said no, he replied, "Good; we need you to be the tenth man." I felt proud, knowing that I could take the role of an adult. I felt that my childhood had ended and that something new—something yet undefined—had begun.

While a bar mitzvah was perceived exclusively as a religious ritual, it was also an occasion for simple presents. For the occasion, my godfather Jozsef Weiss, the owner of the clothing store, gave me a new suit, the first one I ever had. The suit was brown herringbone, with knickers instead of long pants. I was grateful to him for giving me a tangible gift that showed the entire world that I was now a man. Other than the suit, the only gift I received was a set of phylacteries, the little leather cases holding Scriptural passages that Jewish men wear for morning prayers.

After my bar mitzvah, at the age of thirteen and a half, I was sent away to yeshiva in the town of Miskolc, a three hour train ride away. My expenses were covered by an allowance donated by members of the synagogue. My father took me to Rabbi Moishe Yosef Schwartz who lived in a house on a cul-de-sac side street of Miskolc. An overnight train ride had taken me away from home to what felt like the other side of the world. The first Friday I cried inconsolably for two hours. Never again did I cry like that. Deep down, I knew it was the end of my childhood, my expulsion from Eden, and I was not ready for it. I did not know yet what expulsion from Eden and descent into hell actually meant.

The yeshiva was far from magnificent, consisting of one teacher, Rabbi Schwartz, with eight or so students. The teacher lived in a one-room apartment that was divided by sheets from ceiling to floor. His wife was on one side, his books on the other, stacked on a long table. He looked like the saints depicted in nineteenth-century paintings, with a brown beard and saintly eyes. When we arrived, my father said to Rabbi Schwartz, "Here is my son, who is a good student. But he is very bashful; you had better find him places to eat and sleep." So he did. An improvised scholarship system, that worked more or less the same everywhere, had me eat at a different home every day, except on Shabbat eve when I ate with the rabbi, my teacher. We would have soup and chicken and challah. By dinner-time, I was famished. In fact, I was always hungry.

Rabbi Schwartz, a mystic, attended a Hasidic synagogue and, from him, I learned about Hasidism. We often started our day with a ritual bath at four in the morning, followed by the morning service. After we went to synagogue—the service always ran late—we would return home. Rabbi Schwartz would then study until he fell asleep. An hour or so later, he would wake up and sing the *Kiddush,* the special prayer for the Sabbath; then we would have dinner. It was a purely mystical setting led by a sweet, good man. I am now grateful for that unique experience. Everything that one experiences goes into the formation of one's soul.

Going to yeshiva was not preparation for the rabbinate; it was simply something boys did to become a learned Jew and a desirable candidate for marriage. Most boys married soon after leaving yeshiva, at nineteen or twenty, to girls who were sixteen or so. Then the boys would find a trade, which might be anything from chicken farming to trading in feathers or hides or lumber. A few, of course, became rabbis. Some never became anything much, and were like professional graduate students who go from fellowship to fellowship, perhaps writing a monograph now and then. In those days, the poor Jewish scholar was a common phenomenon; some Yiddish writers protested against the yeshivas turning out what they called *Luftmensh*, men expected to make their livings out of thin air.

I never gave any thought to what I would do with my life; it was an abstract subject. That was the first time I had been away from home, and, not being an aggressive person, I never took control of my own situation. I did not do my part to make it a successful experience and, hence, it was not successful: hungry, homesick and jaundiced from a poor diet, I returned home after only four months.

When I came back to Derecske, my father would not talk to me. He had liked the fact that I was a good student and recognized instinctively that learning would be my future. I think he hoped that I might go to Pressburg, believed to be the finest Hungarian yeshiva, for rabbinical training. However, there was no planning for such an outcome; my parents were not those kind of people. Though my father never verbalized his feelings, I felt his deep disappointment. It was as though I had entered Harvard Law School and flunked out after the first quarter. He was a very simple man with an absolute commitment to a few fundamental principles that made sense to him and held his life together, based on his understanding of Orthodox Judaism. The joy and delight of his life was the synagogue. Everything else was incidental.

The time after I returned was a vague, floating, shifting kind of time. I was fifteen years old and should have been in high school, but my family was too poor to send me. I was studying and not studying. My time was difficult, completely unstructured, both night and day. It was an intermission between the past and an uncertain future.

Chapter Three

The World Changed

Anti-Jewish feelings were present in Derecske. While no official ghetto existed, most Jewish homes clustered around the synagogue. Since Jews earned their livings as shopkeepers, they interacted with non-Jewish farmers and artisans daily. In addition, the fact that so many Jewish families lived above or behind their Main Street shops meant that isolation from the rest of the population was minimal. Unlike much of Eastern Europe at that time, Hungarian Jews could own property—though few actually did. Even the synagogue owned land, the result of a national program that gave land to religious institutions.

While the professional lives of Jews intersected with non-Jews, their personal lives did not. I wasn't forbidden to socialize with non-Jews. Nor was it a question of not wanting to. The Jewish community strictly followed the rules of Orthodox religious conduct and its dietary rules and this behavior more than anything else prevented any real social contact with non-Jews. If I could not eat the food served in a gentile house, it would be hard for me to go there. Practically speaking, I could hardly develop a real friendship with a non-Jew if I couldn't visit his or her home for a meal. I never played with a non-Jewish child; I never even had a conversation with a non-Jewish child. Furthermore, I didn't question it: our lives simply didn't intersect.

While I do not remember overt hostility from non-Jews nor do I recall a conscious feeling of being hated yet, I know underlying anti-Jewish feelings existed. Though I do not personally recall ever hearing an anti-Semitic remark or experiencing an unpleasant incident, I learned after the war that many of my friends do. They remember street fights with non-Jewish boys on the way to and from school. They remember market days after a big snow, when a few ruffians would throw hard snowballs at a bearded Jew. But not even at the height of the war was the synagogue defaced or the windows broken. Perhaps later, under Nazi occupation, those things may have happened, but I was in Budapest at the time.

Not much set us apart from the rest of the population. Only a few Jews wore distinctive clothes. As boys we didn't wear yarmulkes, but instead wore soft cloth caps, like golf caps, but this was not unusual as most non-Jewish males also wore caps or hats. When boys became teenagers, they set aside their short pants and put on long pants and a hat.

Jews throughout Hungary engaged in many of the civil activities of the country, including military service. Jews, enfranchised by the Emperor Franz Josef in the 1860s, participated in elections. They were involved in every profession and could own land. However, after Hungary's loss in World War I, anti-Semitism increased significantly in the 1930s and the Hungarian government passed legislation to restrict Jewish freedoms. Law No. XV of 1938, purportedly passed to protect Hungary's social and economic balance, restricted Jewish membership in the professions—law, medicine, engineering, the press, theater, and movies—to twenty percent. Until the ratio of twenty percent was achieved in total membership, not more than five percent of new members could be Jewish. This law, introduced by the Prime Minister and supported by representatives of organized churches, was overwhelmingly approved in both houses of the national legislature. Under its provisions, fifteen thousand Jews in professional occupations were expected to lose their jobs within five years.

Hungarian Jewish leaders accepted the restrictions, believing that these restrictions would prevent more restrictive ones from being enacted. The anti-Semites, they thought, would be satisfied and not press for further change. Of course, they were quickly proven wrong. The next year, 1939, a law entitled "Concerning the Restriction of the Participation of Jews in Public and Economic Life," was enacted that defined "a Jew" —anyone with one Jewish parent or two Jewish grandparents. This new law also declared Jews ineligible to become citizens by naturalization or marriage, barred them from holding any governmental position, and forced the retirement of Jewish court personnel, primary and secondary school teachers, and notaries public. Jews could not be editors or publishers of any periodicals or producers or directors of films or plays. Jews could not buy or sell land without special permission and could be forced to sell or lease their land on terms dictated by authorities. Companies with fewer than five employees could hire only one Jew; companies with nine employees, two. These provisions brought a growing sense of emotional and economic restriction that primarily affected small businessmen and shopkeepers and the workers they employed. Many people lost their jobs.

In the previous years, there had been a gradual but limited disenfranchisement. The most obvious sign came when Jewish boys were no longer obliged— or had the right—to serve in the military. A law passed in March 1939 created a system of conscripted labor whereby Jewish men would assist the Hungarian military—they could be drafted to work for the army—but could not be a member of the army. The oldest of my second cousins, Moishe Aaron, served in a labor battalion and never returned. For a time, we got mail from him. The arrival of letters from family members at the front gave us one of the few joys we had during that cruel time. The letters didn't tell us much, but any sign of life was reassuring. My aunt sent him foodstuffs in cans, rich meats like goose and liver, wonderful baked goods, and beautiful sweaters, but I'm sure they never got to him. After the war, we learned from the few survivors that the Hungarian soldiers confiscated everything worthwhile.

A desire to reverse the pattern of Jewish assimilation into Hungarian life led to further legislative action. In the summer of 1941, the Hungarian Legislature enacted further anti-Jewish legislation based on the Nuremberg Law, specifically banning marriage and sexual relations between Jews and non-Jews. It was an important step in creating an atmosphere that allowed the Nazis to carry out their programs of deportation and extermination.

The anti-Semitic legislation was passed with the acquiescence, even the reluctant approval, of the leadership of the Hungarian Jewish community. Each time, the Jewish leaders accepted the idea that the latest measure would be the last; they believed that the radicals would be satisfied and that small measures of discrimination would protect them from larger ones. They may have been naïve. They may have been self-deluded, but in the long run they were just helpless.

I knew nothing of these laws at the time.

Looking back, one of the most tragic aspects of this time was the nature of the slow and careful annihilation of Hungary's Jews. It was not criminals who took away our civil rights. Rather, the state *legally* confiscated our rights, one by one, until nothing was left.

When the Germans occupied Hungary in March 1944, the Hungarian government cooperated with the Germans in the deportation of its Jewish citizens. Preexisting anti-Jewish feelings were cultivated by German intervention. The ground may have been fertile, but the systematic campaign against the Jews was the product of Nazi programs initiated during the war. Hungary could not have taken these anti-Semitic measures if it had not been for the German occupation. At the same time, I do not exempt Hungary from responsibility for its actions. While most of European Jewry in lands under German occupation was long gone and Polish Jewry decimated by 1943, Hungarian Jewry was still intact. We were the last to go.

At the time, my family and I were not aware of the changes in the political climate. My world was unconnected to the world beyond our borders and life in Derecske went on very much as it had before. We were at the low end of the economic and social structure. Times were hard for us and the legal restrictions did not touch us directly. My father had an increasingly hard time getting jobs, but this did not penetrate my consciousness very deeply. During those early days, I heard my father and his friends talk as they sat around the pot-bellied stove in the synagogue, but I didn't understand what they were saying and had only a vague sense that disturbing things were happening.

After the March 1938 Nazi annexation of Austria, the Anschluss, a new Polish-Hungarian border was established, but that meant nothing to me. At that time, Jewish soldiers had been part of the army that went into Transylvania, Slovakia, and Serbia to repossess lands lost after World War I. In 1940 and 1941, Jewish soldiers were drafted to serve as part of labor battalions primarily on the eastern front. In my mind, that was the beginning of the destruction of our community. Able-bodied men of military age, including some of my cousins, were drafted and many never returned. As I learned later, it was no doubt intended that they be worked, literally, to death. They were employed by the corps of engineers to build tank traps, clear mine fields, and perform all the heavy labor that was required by a great army.

I did, of course, have some knowledge of the war from the time it was declared in September 1939. One day on my way home from school—I was eleven years old—I saw a group of neighbors huddled under the window of a house on Main Street. From inside the house, a radio blared into the street that war had been declared. Germany had invaded Poland. Like Austria, like Czechoslovakia, Poland was far away, so the news meant nothing to me.

When the Germans invaded Norway in May 1940, I remember my father said, "Wait until the French and the British come; they will give the Germans a *potch* (a slap)!" He and his friends were naïve, of course, and I was totally uninformed. Little solid information was available. We had no electricity and no radio. I never saw a newspaper in our house. I never saw a book there either except the prayer book. The only library available to us was the synagogue's collection of religious and liturgical books. In that way, we lived in a narrow intellectual ghetto—an island with precious little communication with the rest of the world.

After the war began, anti-Semitism was expressed more directly. The Hungarian Nazis, referred to as the Arrow Cross based on the shape of their emblem, opened a local headquarters cater-cornered across the street from our Derecske synagogue. Its presence on that site was deliberate; it was clear and silent intimidation. For quite a while, they did little.

In the spring of 1942, there was an overture of more drastic actions to come. One Friday, the rabbi and quite a number of our Jewish community's leading elderly citizens, including my father, were called to the city hall building where their beards were forcibly shorn. The act was an irreverent desecration and cruel psychological warfare. Our basic dignity had been assaulted and I, along with the rest of our community, was shocked. As I watched the rabbi and the other men arrive at the synagogue that night, I felt as though I were witnessing the destruction of the ancient temple in Jerusalem. The act was concrete and chilling. I felt as though we had all been raped.

During 1942 and 1943, the Jews in Hungary were in limbo. I was working. Synagogues and businesses were open. Everything was semi-normal. We did not have the burning of synagogues that I later learned occurred in Germany. Hungary's Jewish leaders may have known what was happening to Jews in Poland and were torn by what they knew, but we knew nothing. I cannot help but wonder—what would have happened if they had alerted the entire Jewish community and said, *We are in great danger. There is a policy of extermination in the eastern lands. The Germans are misleading us and we must resist with all our power and in whatever way we can.* What would have happened then? Would history have been any different?

What did the adults in our community know and not want to tell the children? My mother used to make strange noises in response to rumors of the burnings of bodies. One local man, a member of a labor battalion in the Ukraine, came back on leave and informed his family about Jews being killed in a mass grave. I have later wondered since—could it have been Babi Yar?

The first time I saw German soldiers was in Derecske, probably in 1943 before I moved to Budapest. A regiment marched through town and I was impressed because they appeared to be very sharp soldiers. From the perspective of a village boy, the tanks, trucks, and equipment were dazzling. Everything was shiny and polished and the soldiers were the picture of health, like an ancient Roman legion. Pictures of bedraggled soldiers on the front line that are familiar to many are nothing like what I saw that day. The Germans exuded a spirit of invincibility. They were going through to the East and stayed overnight, parking their vehicles in the central market place. I can still see the tanks perfectly lined up.

Chapter Four

Budapest

By 1943, my father could no longer piece together enough work in Derecske to support our family and so, when I was fifteen, my father and I and my two sisters, Ilona and Iren, moved to Budapest to seek work. The beginning of the war had worsened my family's situation that was already bad.

When I debarked from the train in Budapest at the great Eastern railroad station, a splendid, monumental building, I stood for a long time at the head of a long flight of stairs. Below me lay a great circle, where the trolleys came from every direction like the spokes of a wheel. For a country boy who had just come to the city, to simply stand at the top of the stairs and see the activity was exciting beyond words. I had left my rural town behind me and had finally entered the world I had always imagined I wanted. A world of freedom, movement, and change. Budapest was an astonishingly beautiful world. A world for which I was not the least bit prepared.

While being near the capital offered an opportunity to discover an entirely new world, I was not able to take advantage of what the city had to offer. I had no money and no one to introduce me to the life of the city. I did not even know what possibilities existed. I was like a child pressing his face against a department store window, looking through the glass but unable to enter.

My father had secured a job as a registrar of graves at the central Jewish cemetery in Budapest. There were 330,000 Jews in Budapest, so the operation was quite sophisticated. The cemetery was enormous and had a staff of more than six hundred people, a smaller scale version of Arlington National Cemetery. It had twelve greenhouses and its own botanical and horticultural staff to raise the flowers and decorative plants for the graves and landscaping. I found a happy niche working as an apprentice botanist in this unit owned and managed by the Holy Society whose primary responsibility was the

25

maintenance of the Jewish cemeteries in Budapest. I started by watering the plants and learning how to plant seedlings in flowerbeds. The work was good for me, vigorous, outdoor work that made me physically strong, crucial in my later struggle to survive. I was already accustomed to tough conditions—the circumstances of my youth having made me hardy—but I became even stronger through my work. Many boys who had been raised in gentler circumstances did not survive the concentration camps.

Ilona and Iren, my two older sisters, found work in Budapest as nannies and lived with the families they worked for. My father and I lived in staff housing on the edge of the cemetery. We did our own simple cooking and sent money back to my mother to support her and my younger brother and sister who had stayed behind in Derecske. My family had broken up, but that was not uncommon for the time.

Living in the quiet Budapest suburb that we did, my father and I did not belong to an organized Jewish community. Part of the difficulty of that time for us was being cut off from our religious foundation. This isolation was particularly hard for my father, being at heart a rural Jew accustomed to the close proximity and warmth of our Derecske Jewish community. Occasionally, we would celebrate Sabbath in the home of a local man who couldn't travel and those evenings alleviated some of the pain of our isolation.

But my father did seem to find something else to identify with: after a few months of living in Budapest, my father announced that he was a Social Democrat. I did not know what that meant at the time but, later when I did understand, I was impressed with his new engagement with the broader world. He began reading the *Nepszava*, the "People's Voice," the newspaper of the Social Democratic Party.

During my free time, I rode the trolley into Budapest to visit some of the city's great synagogues, but I still felt as though I was an outsider, a rootless, country boy. I took enormous pleasure from listening to the cantors at the Rumbach Street Synagogue. The building was a fantastic work of art: its architecture a visual delight. The cantors at the cemetery introduced me to the choir director at the great synagogue, and, prior to the Nazi occupation of the city, I had auditioned for and been accepted into the choir. While I did not study singing until I came to the United States, I had a natural talent for it, inherited from my mother who had a wonderful voice. The Jewish culture is one that appreciates singing and the art of Jewish folk music was mine. As a youngster, I had sung at home and in the synagogue. We had sung at every occasion—at the Seder table, at Sabbath services, all holidays.

But when I appeared for the first rehearsal on March 20th, everyone had disappeared. I shelved my musical plans and continued to raise flowers. Forty years later, I met the cantor's son in Washington and learned they had gone into hiding.

Reading the daily newspapers was a critical development for me that began around this time. According to my sister Ilona, I always had two newspapers in my pocket. By then, my curiosity about the world's events began and I specifically wanted to read about the war. I spent hours in the theaters watching newsreels. They were obviously propagandistic, showing the heroic battles, the triumphs of the Axis Powers, and the meeting between Hitler and Mussolini at the Brenner Pass.

During this time, I strayed from my Orthodox background more than I had previously. (My first attempt to assert my independence happened several years earlier when I was about eleven: I cut off the *pais* (earlocks) that I had worn as a boy. My father, predictably, was furious and slapped me across the face.)

Our society was one in which religious symbols were very powerful. Orthodox Jews knew that a rejection of the symbols meant a rejection of the tradition. If one questioned any of the traditions, the entire structure became fragile, vulnerable to outside attack. Everyone understood the basic tenets: God was at the center of our world. Life was basically good, although one was obliged to struggle. One worked hard to put food on the table. One lived as an honorable person and a good Jew, teaching one's children to live life in the same way, trying to live in peace, working out ways to co-exist with secular authority. So, while in Budapest, when I began to go to the movies with one of my sisters on Saturday afternoons, I was emotionally conflicted. Simply getting to the theater was a transgression because we had to go by trolley, a violation of the Sabbath laws we had always observed at home.

Budapest was beautiful in the spring and summer of 1944. Even though the war was in its fifth year, Budapest was still essentially untouched, radiantly beautiful. I had been an apprentice botanist for more than a year, raising geraniums, begonias, and coleus in the Jewish cemetery. My father continued to work as a grave registrar. My sisters Iren and Ilona still worked as nannies.

Despite the beauty of the city, darkness descended for Hungarian Jews in March with the German occupation of the entire country and the arrival of Adolph Eichmann's death machinery in Budapest. I saw German troops everywhere in the capital, visible in significant numbers in the coffee houses and along the boulevards. If a formal announcement of the occupation had been made, I was unaware of it.

With the German occupation, our situation quickly became serious. The first direct and immediate impact of German occupation was the wearing of the yellow star. When the order came out that Jews had to wear yellow stars, we bought yellow cloth, made the stars, and sewed them on our outer garments. This didn't actually seem so terrible to me, because Jewish men of military age, instead of wearing uniforms, wore civilian clothes with yellow armbands. I had an adolescent's ignorance of the implications of such things. I still have a picture of my father in which you can see the star quite clearly.

The mood had shifted and steps were taken against Jewish businesses. One day, most Jewish-owned businesses in Budapest were confiscated. However, the company I worked for was not affected: people had to bury their dead.

Periodically the police raided the markets. If you were shopping in the market, wearing a star, that was the end of you. Officially, customers needed coupons to buy the rationed bread. However, bakers made extra money by baking extra bread and charging more for it. I would buy several loaves of bread and walk to where my sister worked and lived, only a few blocks from the market. My heart pounded with fear. While buying bread without the necessary coupon was clearly dangerous, it was also an adventure, an act of defiance and daring.

Some Jews went outdoors without the star. The father of one of my friends tore off his star and replaced it with a red, white and green armband to make it appear as though he were a member of the civil defense unit. He was an adult and knowledgeable about the ways of the world and could take a step such as this to protect himself. My father, sisters and I were not that knowledgeable. We were like rabbits in a field with no place to hide; eagles could just swoop down and take us.

The mail from Derecske stopped coming. We were benumbed and depressed by the war and accepted the cessation of contact with our family in Derecske with an air of 'What else is new?'

I had no contact with anyone who might have known anything. I was not a part of the Budapest Jewish community, nor was I part of my hometown anymore. I am embarrassed now to think of how uninformed, naïve, and intellectually isolated I was. Still an immature country boy, my interests were not focused on politics. Even the arrival of German troops in Budapest did not make a strong impression on me. Today this couldn't happen; a teenager would be more aware. He would know about resistance movements and would perhaps get involved in one.

I am now enraged whenever I think of this: When I look back on myself and my father, I grow angry over the passivity that our isolation and religious conditioning encouraged. *How could I not have known anything, suspected anything? How could my father not tell me anything? What did my father know?*

I was a chicken waiting to be plucked. In the long run, however, it didn't make any difference. What if I had known of all the terrifying possibilities? I would have gone insane or I would have tried something foolish and gotten myself killed. What real possibilities existed for me?

The people I now have sympathy for were those who may have known, adults with wives and children and elderly parents. How must they have felt? What must they have thought?

While the time was tough for all, at least I worked in a place that I loved, a Jewish enterprise, among Jews, so there was no harassment at work. I was optimistic that the war would soon be over. June 6, 1944—D-Day—was a gorgeous day and my hopes were high. With two newspapers in my hand, with their blazing headlines—"Allies Land in France," I hoped for a quick victory. By then, of course, we had no illusions about the Nazis and their anti-Semitism, but we hoped a quick Allied victory would rescue us. I remember the adults talking about this, with my dad speaking about Churchill and Roosevelt and what they were going to do. The news we received was censored so we never really knew how the armies were faring. I remember peeking through the windows of the bookstores on Elizabeth Avenue that were full of books about Rommel, "The Hero of Africa."

By this time, the Jews had no question of divided loyalty. Patriotism to our mother country no longer mattered; only survival mattered. Hungary was under military occupation, so we looked to the West for deliverance. There had always been an orientation toward the West, now embodied in the Allied powers. The United States—Washington D.C.—became the beacon of hope. The White House was a mystical place, a holy of holies. The raging battles in France after D-Day and in Russia marked the beginning of the end for the Nazis. However, my own battle for survival was about to begin.

During the spring of 1944, my mother came to visit us in Budapest. She carried with her a quiet dignity; she was one of the poor who suffered quietly. She was very intelligent and must have had great strength. She could sing with joy even at the worst of times, even when she was begrudged her crust of bread. I have often wondered what her feelings must have been, separated from most of her family. I assume it was hard for my father as well, seeing his family broken apart. I understand from friends that she encouraged others, helping them and telling then not to worry. It seemed as though she could cope with anything.

I think she realized when she came to Budapest that she would not see us again. She must have been desperate to see my father one more time and was ready to make any sacrifice to do so. The trip had to have been very difficult, overnight on the train on hard benches. She didn't want to travel alone, so she brought my brother with her. She and my father were then in their late 40's. They must have been in terrible anguish. The visit lasted a couple of days and was largely a silent meeting; I do not remember a single conversation. My mother did not say anything to me about their circumstances, though I am sure she and my father talked.

Suddenly, in June, we lost contact with her and the rest of the family at home and for some time we were totally ignorant of their fate.

Chapter Five

Arrest and Deportation

Sunday July 8, 1944 was a glistening, summer day. An American air raid the previous night had produced many casualties that overwhelmed the facilities of the Jewish cemetery. The regular staff was no longer at full strength because some of the Jews had already gone into hiding; as a result, I was asked to help with the burial of a young man who had been killed in the air raid. I did not know it at the time but, by the end of June, over 381,000 Hungarian Jews, half of Hungary's Jewish citizens, had been deported to Auschwitz.

The man to be buried, a member of the Jewish labor service, was young, probably in his early twenties. His wife—young and pregnant—and her parents attended the burial. I will never forget her—a beautiful woman who must have been at least six months pregnant. When the service, conducted at the central cemetery chapel, was completed, several men placed the casket on a caisson that another man pulled to the gravesite.

At the end of the funeral, Hungarian gendarmes appeared and ordered us to assemble at the main gate. My father, my two sisters who happened to be visiting us from the city that day, myself, and about fifteen others were lined up at the gate and were marched off without explanation to a military compound.

I remember nothing of the trip there.

Once inside the compound, we were taken to a building somewhat like a large open-door garage with no windows. A few hundred people who had similarly been rounded up off the streets of Budapest were already there.

The building was isolated from public view. A machine gun mounted on a tripod stood in the opening facing us, but I don't recall that a guard was stationed there all the time. The building was in the middle of an enclosed military stockade, so the Hungarian soldiers didn't have to do anything to guard us. There was nowhere to go.

It was hot and people were crying.

If we received any food, I don't remember.

There were no toilet facilities; I don't know how we took care of bathroom needs.

No one spoke. I don't know whether everyone was in shock or simply chose to keep their thoughts to themselves.

There was no coordination, no organization among those of us held in the stockade.

No one took charge.

We were each on our own.

We spent the night there—a mass of bodies attempting to sleep on a hard concrete floor.

The next day, we were taken by barge down the Danube to a brick factory. About eight hundred people had already been brought to this concentration point, which was guarded by Hungarian soldiers.

It was still very, very hot. Once there, the soldiers made my father remove his hat—a kind of torture in the unbearable beating heat of the summer sun.

When I entered the building, I descended into an unspeakable situation. The sight of people—old and young, men, women, and children—dazed, sitting on the bare ground in an abandoned brick factory shocked me beyond belief. Walking through the facility, I heard screaming and moaning and realized in horror that people were being tortured. Later I understood that the guards, primarily Hungarian, with a handful of SS soldiers mixed in, were trying to discover the hidden location of money and valuables of those people they had captured. This was the first time I encountered a member of Hitler's SS. I remember one SS soldier with a cocky hat and a frightening pistol at his side. He beat people at random with a whip. He exuded brutality.

Only a few days earlier, these human beings had lived under civilized conditions, yet they were now stripped of every shred of their personal dignity. In an instant, their humanity was stolen.

I was sixteen years old and I shall never forget the cruelty of that day.

The first day there, or perhaps the second or third, as I wandered around in boredom, I came upon a line of about fifty people in front of an office, probably what had been a foreman's office during an earlier time when the brick factory was in operation.

I asked a man in line, "Where are you going? Why are you lined up?"

He answered, "We were arrested on the trolley car in the city and are permitted to return home to get our personal belongings." I instinctively lied, saying that I too had been arrested on the trolley car. I joined the line, not thinking about where I was going or whether I would come back. Just to be away for a day was reason enough to stand in that line. The guards who were to accompany us back into Budapest designated a subway station and a specified time for us to return. We had to give our names and addresses. I was gullible and thought it made sense. I didn't have time to tell my father what I was doing, which concerned me, but I went anyway because I thought it might be an opportunity to obtain food. I didn't yet realize that finding food would be one of my biggest challenges in the coming months.

I took the trolley and went back to our neighborhood. I found a man I knew, a non-Jew who worked for the cemetery taking care of horses. He was roasting a couple of hares on a spit. I bought two loaves of bread and a hare from him and returned. When I arrived at the agreed-upon subway station, the soldier was waiting. He said nothing. Few others came. I'm sure that the soldiers had taken bribes from the others. The guards never passed up an opportunity to line their own pockets. Finally, he simply said, "I guess this is all," and we took the trolley back to the brick factory.

I felt foolish for returning, but I had to see my father again; he did not know where I was and I didn't want him to worry about me. It was a frightening time: where would I have gone? I would have felt terribly guilty about abandoning my father and sisters. We were very close. I couldn't do that. I was glad that I had gone back.

I returned by sunset with the bread and the entirely not kosher roasted rabbit. I told Dad where I had been and showed him the bread and rabbit. We ate the food without speaking of the sacrilege we were committing. It no longer mattered.

The following morning was the beginning of one of the saddest days of my life.

The brickyard where we had been brought had a railroad siding convenient for transport. My father, my sisters and I, and everyone else were loaded onto a long freight train made up of boxcars. Guards opened boxcar after boxcar and shoved people in until each was full. Our train held about three thousand. Even now I wonder how the old people managed to get onto the train: the floors of the cars were very high off the ground.

The unexpected, sudden brutal treatment was stunning and demoralizing. One month earlier, on D-Day, June 6 when the U.S. and British troops stormed the beaches of Normandy, I was walking on Elizabeth Boulevard in Budapest, reading a newspaper. June 6th had been a beautiful day and I was free and full of hope. I may have been hungry and I may have had only one suit to my name, but I was free. A month later I was a prisoner in a place unspeakable for its horrors, treated worse than an unwanted, caged animal.

I now wonder if my rootless and transitory days in Budapest away from my mother, away from my extended family and my closely-knit Jewish community, helped prepare me psychologically for deportation and what came after. I no longer had a home rooted in community and love. Though I was with my father and two of my sisters were nearby, my family had already been torn apart and I had been separated from my childhood home and the people I loved. I think if I had had to make that endless, dark trip in the boxcar with everyone I knew from Derecske, instead of with strangers as I did, I would have been more emotionally devastated when I arrived. Even so the trip was one of the most horrendous experiences of my life.

The doors of the boxcars were locked and the transport began to roll to an unknown destination. As many as ninety people were in each boxcar that had one small window, perhaps a couple of square feet, at each end.

The inside of the car was always in semi-darkness.

We were sealed in, in the heat of the summer, without food or water. Old and young packed together. My father and sisters were in the same car; we were determined to stay together as long as we could.

Night and day the train rushed with unusual speed, as if it were on an exceptionally important mission.

I remember the terrible fatigue, terrible heat and terrible thirst—thirst above all.

I remember the unbearable uncertainty, not knowing where we were going or what waited at the end.

Looking out the window near the top of the boxcar, I could see the beautiful countryside rush by. I looked out at the green rolling hills and blooming fruit trees; the scenery was lush and gorgeous, but the only names we could see were strange and difficult to read as the train hurried toward its destination. We didn't know where we were. Years later I realized that beautiful terrain was Slovakia.

Inside the car, anxiety and fear exhausted us into a state of half-sleep. How could this happen? I was pessimistic about the outcome, but I had no idea just how bad it would be.

While still in Hungary, Hungarian soldiers had participated in our deportation. However, once across the Hungarian border into Czechoslovakia, in a town called Kassa, the German guards replaced the Hungarian soldiers.

From time to time, the train would stop but the guards never came into the cars; perhaps they were afraid to. The soldiers asked people to throw out their valuables. They threatened us—"Do you have anything that should not be taken out of the country? It is your life that is at stake!" If we did not give them our possessions we would be shot.

Through the small window, I watched in terror one man—perhaps because he seemed prosperous or looked like a leader—beaten unmercifully with a stick. They almost broke his back.

We had room in the boxcars to sit, but not to lie down. The floor was bare wood. There was nothing on the floor; some had blankets to rest on but my family had nothing.

People stood. They sat.

Nobody talked much. I can't remember a single conversation, fight or quarrel, though I remember what I was thinking: *Where are we going? What is going to happen to us? What town is this? Are we going East? South?*

Being near the little windows at each end was the best place. People quietly took turns to breathe a bit of fresh air and to catch a glimpse of the world passing by.

We slept a great deal of time out of sheer depression.

The trip took about four days.

The heat was oppressive.

The stench unbearable.

Our thirst indescribable.

We longed for little: Fresh air, water, and the ability to stretch our legs.

Synagogue—Derecske, Hungary

Derecske Main Street

Kati, my sister; Zseni, my mother; Sandor, my brother—1944

Ilona, my sister; Herman, my father; Iren, my sister; and me—1944

Rabbi Hisrch Kohn of Derecske

Arthur Rubin and Jack Margarten, age 13, at Arthur's Bar Mitzvah—1941

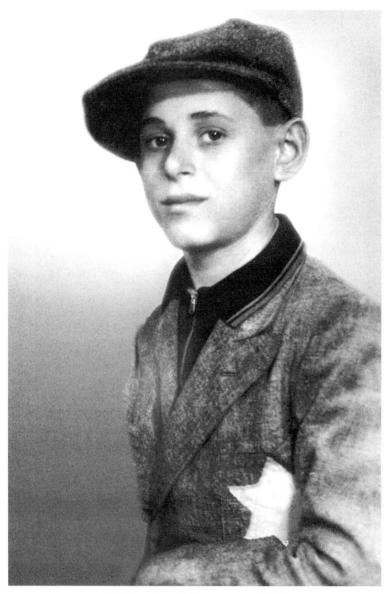

Laszlo at Age 16, in Budapest—1944

Deportation of Arthur Rubin's Family to Ghetto—June 1944

Arrival at Auschwitz-Birkenau

Jewish Men of Derecske in Forced Labor Camp, Hungary—1944

Remnants of barracks at Auschwitz-Birkenau—2002

Camp Wobbelin—US Army Photo May 1945

Liberated Prisoners—Camp Wobbelin—May 1945, US Army Photo

Liberation, May 2nd, 1945 with the 82nd Airborne Division

Arrival in Halsingborg, Sweden, Circa July 1945

Lunch Time with Nurses in Sweden—1945

Laszlo, Jack, Arthur with Group—Sweden, 1945

Laszlo One Year After Liberation—1946

Laszlo on the Ski Slopes—Sweden

School in Visingso, Sweden—1946

School Picture, Visingso, Sweden—1946

Arthur Rubin—1946

Laszlo and Jack, Sweden—1946

Jack Margareten—1946, Sweden

Elizabeth (Baba) Mohr, Favorite Teacher in Sweden

Laszlo Front Row Left—Soccer Team—Visingso, Sweden—1946

Ilona, daughter Aniko, son, Sandor and Husband Laszlo Frank Post War Hungary

Iren, husband Aryeh Katz, daughter Shoshonah and son,
Moshe (Moti), Gedera, Israel—1960

*Laszlo with Imre Zwiebel on Ship in Atlantic
to New York—January 1948*

PFC Laszlo Berkowits as Chaplain's Assistant with Chaplain Samuel Soble—
Shabbat Service —Hickam Air Force Base—Honolulu, Hawaii—1956

Scofield Barracks, Honor Guard—1955 PFC Berkowits

Photo Taken for Application to Hebrew Union College—1956

Wedding Reception, Dec 27, 1961. Dr. Zoltan Fried, Renee and Henry Friedman,
Arthur Rubin, Judith Ann Berkowits and Laszlo

Frank L. Weil, Chairman of Board of HUC—with President Truman

*Laszlo's Ordination as Rabbi, with Rabbis Dr. Nelson Gluck,
Dr. Alexander Scheiber—1963*

Laszlo's In-laws from left to right, Max and Hilda Mitman, Dennis, Joan, and Judith Mitman

Rabbi Berkowits, Temple Rodef Shalom, Falls Church, VA—1972

Sam Glueck from Derescke—1980

Laszlo with Moshe Weiss and Shaiko Aron in Israel—1982

Rabbi Officiating at Wedding of Temple Member

*82nd Airborn Members at Temple Rodef Shalom in 1995—
50th Anniverary of Liberation*

Senior Rabbi—Temple Rodef Shalom, Falls Church, VA, 1963–1998

Eli Wiesel at Temple Rodef Shalom

Laszlo with President George H. Bush—Hanukah at the White House—1989

Laszlo and Wife Judy—1998 (Married in Cincinnati, 1961)

Julie Berkowits with husband Peter Poggioli, daughter Zoe, and son Sam—2007

Deborah Berkowits with husband Rabbi Alan Litwak, and daughters (from left) Yael, Hannah and Naomi

Chapter Six

Arrival

The train came to a halt on a railroad siding without a name. None of us knew where we were or what would happen to us. Loud voices in a foreign language that sounded like Yiddish but I suspected was German penetrated the stifling air of the still-sealed freight car. Suddenly, the sliding door scraped open and orders rang out: "Aussteigen." I knew no German at that time, but the meaning was obvious enough—"Get out!" Peering out, we could see SS troops, with huge German shepherd dogs at their sides, patrolling the vicinity. Men, obviously prisoners, in strange striped clothing helped us climb down from the wagons. They spoke in all the tongues of the German-occupied lands. I found out later what they were saying: "Leave your belongings. You will get them later." I had nothing with me to leave.

Exhausted from the brutal journey, we did as we were told. I was relieved that the trip was over. In my innocence, I was hopeful that whatever came next would be better than the trip that brought us there. I think others shared the same sense of relief. Worn down from the transport and the heat, I was grateful to be out of the wagon, able to stand on firm ground. I was dirty, hungry, and thirsty, desperate for a drink of water.

Once on the ground, my relief vanished. I faced an unworldly spectacle. I didn't have any idea what it was all about but it was immediately clear we had been brought to a huge prison. I saw a vast expanse filled with long wooden barracks, surrounded by a tall fence constructed of barbed wire strung on gigantic concrete posts twenty feet apart. Guards with machine guns were on elevated watchtowers. The guns shouted their intentions.

The prison went on and on, as far as I could see. A prison, as I would discover, unlike any other in the world. Inside, I saw thousands of men wandering, seemingly in a daze.

Nothing in my sixteen years had prepared me for this.

Processing began immediately, in great haste and with much weeping and protestation. A tall man dressed in a spit-and-polished officer's uniform, a man who I later learned was Jozef Mengele, separated people. The very old and very young, mothers with young children, pregnant women and the infirm, moved ever so slowly to the other side of the ramp, toward a wooded area.

Men and women were separated, families broken. Young, able-bodied women unencumbered by a child, including my sisters, were sent to one side. I couldn't see which way they were going but I called out my goodbye to Iren and Ilona. "See you later." I never imagined that later would mean sixteen years for Iren and twenty-one years for Ilona.

None of us cried; we were too dazed to grasp what might be happening.

Father stayed by my side.

The men were lined up army style.

The line moved quickly.

Then it was my turn. As I faced the SS officer, he asked my age. "Sixteen," I replied. My father and I were admitted to the camp, judged capable of useful work.

The SS processed all three thousand in less than an hour.

I went with the men, who were then separated into two groups, one sent to the right, one to the left.

My father and I were sent to the left. We, the able-bodied ones, the ones sent to the left, marched into camp toward a building, into one tremendous room where our clothing was taken away. Many people had come in their best clothes, often with blankets and comforters. We stood naked in front of barbers who cut all our body hair, including our pubic hair. The hair cutting was humiliating and dehumanizing, but it was over quickly. The barbers, prisoners themselves, went about their work as indifferently as if they had been sheering sheep. They used barber's shears and worked without talking, telling us nothing.

I was devastated when I later saw our beautiful women, women of all ages, shorn of their hair.

We were then moved into a vast room to take a shower. The smell of chlorine, heavy in the air, was unfamiliar and contributed to the strange, alienating experience. I remembered our sweet Hungarian water.

We were not allowed to talk during the haircutting and showering. I don't remember anybody talking to me. The only words spoken were orders given in German by the guards.

At the far end of the barracks, after the shower, they gave us blue and white striped prison uniforms of a scratchy, coarse fabric. Different sizes must have been on hand, because mine fit me well enough. We were allowed to keep our shoes and socks.

At that juncture, we marched into what I learned later was Camp E. Along with all the other teenage boys and their fathers, I was separated from my father who was placed in another section, or block as they were known, of the same camp.

It was late at night by the time I was assigned to Block 11, Camp E. My block was already filled with close to one thousand teenage boys from Hungary who had arrived weeks earlier. We were packed in, sardine-fashion, sleeping on three levels of wooden planks. I found an empty spot, and squeezed myself in. Surrounded by hundreds of other boys, I was completely alone. My personal encounter with the most terrible event of the twentieth century had begun. I had entered the universe of the Nazi concentration camp, Auschwitz-Birkenau.

Exhausted, I fell asleep.

Chapter Seven

Auschwitz-Birkenau

Early the next morning, all the prisoners, including me, were lined up between the barracks to be counted. Between each pair of barracks was an open space big enough for two columns of five hundred men to stand, facing each other. The purpose of the roll call was to make sure that no one had escaped. We stood hour after hour in the heat until the soldiers were satisfied.

That first morning during the roll call, I looked across the column facing me and was stunned to see four of my former Derecske schoolmates, Arthur Rubin, Jack Margaretten, Fiuka Sternberger, and Sandor Spitz. "Am I glad to see you!" I said. I couldn't wait to ask them when they had arrived, because I suspected that my mother, brother and sister had come at the same time.

After the roll call was over, when we were given bread and coffee, I had the opportunity to ask about my mother, my sister Kati and brother Sandor. My friends said that they had all arrived together three weeks before, together with our entire Jewish community of Derecske.

I asked, "Where are the mothers and little children?"

They replied, "On the other side of the railroad tracks." For several weeks I believed them: there was, after all, another camp across the tracks.

That day, my friend Arthur gave me the details of what had happened at home on a sunny day in mid-June, the darkest of all days for the Jews of the township. Arthur was heading for morning prayers at six o'clock. As he opened the gate from his yard to the street, he was stopped by an armed policeman and told he could not leave his home.

Soon the police entered his house and gave orders: "You have two hours to pack a few essentials for a trip of three days." Arthur told me that that day his mother had planned to bake bread. Since there was not enough time, they left their home, the dough in its wicker basket. Outside the gate, a horse-drawn cart was waiting for the family to load up. The town council had hired local farmers for that job. "My mother and two younger siblings, already separated from my father, my sisters and myself, were crowded in with the rest," Arthur told me.

Derecske's Jews were torn from the only homes they had ever known. Young and old, infants and schoolchildren, grandmothers and grandfathers were snatched from the home they loved. By this time, June of 1944, many of the local men were already gone, having been conscripted into the forced labor units of the Hungarian army; including Arthur's father, who had left a wife and seven children behind, and Jack's older brothers. At the slow pace of horse-drawn wagons, it took all day to reach the city of Nagyvarad, a ghetto where all the Jews from the outlying villages and towns had been gathered. Crowded into small rooms, they waited fearfully for an unknown future.

After more than a week in the ghetto, on June 26th, they endured a journey similar to mine. They were loaded onto a train of cattle cars, eighty to ninety people in each one. The doors were slammed shut and locked. One small window near the ceiling was the only opening through which a bit of fresh air could enter. Inside the cars, conditions soon became unbearable. Through day and night the train roared toward a destination known only to the Hungarian soldiers and the German SS guards who took over once the train left Hungary.

After a nightmarish three days and nights, the train arrived at Auschwitz-Birkenau. At that time during the summer of 1944, the camp contained its highest concentration of prisoners, approximately 140,000.

I learned quickly that life in camp had a distinct routine.

The *Appel*, the daily counting of prisoners was a unique form of Nazi-designed torture. It took place every morning and every evening without fail, no matter the weather, unbearable heat, pouring rain, or freezing cold. The Germans made a big event of the roll call: we had to stand at attention until an SS soldier counted every single prisoner.

My concerns while enduring the Appel were both small and large. One problem arose if I needed to relieve myself. We weren't allowed to leave. Sometimes boys couldn't control themselves and soiled their clothes. Only after the Appel was complete, could we go to the latrine and wash. The impact was emotionally devastating. However, my greater concern was that I never knew when there might be a "selection," the Nazi determination of who was to die that day.

After the roll call we were given coffee—not real coffee, but something hot that was probably made from licorice. I had been used to an artificial coffee in Hungary, so the poor quality made little difference to me, but the bread was execrable.

Each barrack at Birkenau was the same, a long, low wooden building. The barracks were painted gray, the inside walls whitewashed. Each barrack could contain a thousand people. Down the center of the barracks was a long linear, low brick structure that heated the building in the winter. On either side of it was a narrow aisle with room for one or two people to walk. The rest of the space was taken up by bunks—or, more accurately, tiers of three wooden shelves, set slightly at an angle so one's head was a bit elevated. There were no mattresses, bed linens or blankets. We slept on the boards in the clothes we had worn all day. For light, a narrow horizontal window ran along the base of the ceiling, too high to see anything but a tiny patch of sky. The floors of the barracks were packed dirt. A small room for the barrack supervisor, the *block-alteste*, also a prisoner, was located near the front entrance; the blockalteste was the only person who had any degree of privacy.

For washing, we had only a long, military-style sink with running water. There was no possibility of an actual bath. The shower I took on entering the camp was the last one until liberation—290 days. Any washing of clothes had to be done at the sink; I guess we washed our shirts now and then.

There was no toilet inside the barrack; during the night, boys urinated in a big barrel that was carried away every morning. There was a latrine as big as one of the barracks; perhaps a hundred people could use it at one time, back to back, the whole length of the building. After a while, one thought nothing of it. We would go there to sit and talk during bodily functions. We were glad to be able to sit.

The barracks were only used for sleeping; during daylight hours we were outside. We were only allowed in the barracks during the day when the camp was locked down; during those times, the prisoners were forbidden to leave the barracks. Lockdown occurred during two circumstances: The first was if there had been some sort of disturbance in the camp. The second was if the Allies were flying overhead. The SS did not want the Allies to know how many people were imprisoned in the camps, so any time there was an Allied flight overhead—for example, a raid against the IG Farben chemical plant nearby—we would be locked inside the barracks, hidden from view.

Nobody was known by name. I was never tattooed with a number nor was anyone else in my transport. I do not know why; not being tattooed meant there was no specific plan for me. Jews, political prisoners, criminals, and homosexuals were identified by a colored triangle on their uniforms. By the time I got to Auschwitz, all the political prisoners and homosexuals who had survived were in leadership positions, such as the head of a barrack.

In our building, our blockalteste was a non-Jewish German. He sexually abused two boys in my barracks. At that time I knew nothing of homosexuality; my friends and I thought that the two boys were there to keep his quarters clean. I know that these boys survived; they came to the hospital with me after liberation on May 2, 1945. I was so naïve then; I asked them, "What is the matter with you?" I learned later that they had suffered physically, and I assumed psychologically, from the abuse.

Other block elders were criminals. The foremen among the prisoners were called *capos*; it was a term I had never heard before and only later learned that it was an Italian word. I am sure that the people who became capos, whether they were Jews or not, were brutal men. We had to watch them all the time and stay out of their way and sight, knowing that they were watching us.

I had been separated from my father at our arrival, but soon learned that he was in Camp E with other men, further down the line, about block 8. Physically, it was not that difficult to go to see my father; we were in the same camp. There were no internal barriers; I could just walk over there. While each camp was distinct, separated by barbed wire, within each camp there were about twenty-four barracks in great blocks and the prisoners could roam at will. I was able to visit my father briefly during one of our first days there. We said hello and chatted about nothing much. We had little to say. Something had weakened my emotional ties to my father. As I looked at him, I realized he was no longer the same person. He was quiet, lost in his thoughts.

I have since seen this phenomenon of psychological distancing happen to individuals who have a family member who is terminally ill, a distancing that is essentially an act of self-preservation. I recall one father and son who were with us in the camp who fought with each other terribly especially toward the end, as liberation came nearer. They traded accusations and charges—"Leave me alone; you're killing me."

In hindsight, counterintuitive as it may sound, I have realized that one's chances of survival were far greater if you were not with a member of your family. Seeing a member of your family suffer was a tremendous emotional drain; it added to your own suffering and made you weaker. You could do little or nothing to help him. You were better off with a friend. Unlike many other fathers and sons who were separated and never saw each other again, I did see my father just a few times after that first day. But, one day soon after the first week, without warning, my father was taken away on a workers' transport.

There was no goodbye. I never saw him again. One day he was simply not there anymore. He must have died during the next weeks or months, but I don't know when or where. My father should have survived because he was powerfully built, a strong man physically. But he had been susceptible to respiratory problems, such as the flu or pneumonia. Perhaps that is how he died.

My father's life had been one of constant struggle and he had a tragic ending on top of that life of struggle. He struggled like millions of East Europeans struggled. He had his personal happiness in his children, his family, and his faith. He loved the synagogue and the holidays. For him, to live according to the Torah was deeply satisfying; that was his life. He never dreamed about a big house, a big vacation, a big anything as far as I know. But he certainly would have liked to have lived out his days in peace. In my mind, it is part of his tragedy that even his contented life of poverty was denied him.

In early August 1944, about a month after my arrival, a transport of Jews arrived from the Lodz ghetto of Poland. One of the new arrivals pointed to a nearby building with a tall chimney that was always smoking—sometimes flames shot out of it—and asked me if I knew what happened in that building. I answered, "I think it's a bakery."

The man answered, "You Hungarians are stupid. That building is a crematorium. They burn people there." I had never heard the word crematorium before. The men from Lodz, having already been incarcerated for several years, had learned about the gas chambers and crematoria in other parts of Poland.

I told my friends, "Don't talk to these Polish people; they're so depressing." I simply did not want to believe the man's revelation, but I was scared. In Camp D, adjacent to us, another young man from Derecske, a year older than me, Sam Gluck was imprisoned. He had been assigned to work on the railroad ramp where the transports arrived. Since he mingled with the veteran inmates, I thought he would know the truth. I turned to him to find out the truth about Auschwitz-Birkenau.

I asked him, "Sam, is it true what the Polish guy told me? Is it true that they gassed and burned the people who went to the other side?"

Sam hesitated for a moment then nodded his head in affirmation.

"You mean all our people—your mother and your brothers and sisters, my mother and my brother and sister—were murdered in the gas chamber the day they got here?"

"Yes," he said, "all of them died—men, women, and children—too old or too young for slave labor." They had died in the gas chambers within hours after their arrival.

My family that had stayed behind in Derecske had died that first day, the eighth day of the Hebrew month of Tamuz. Unwillingly, I accepted that awful truth. I thought not only of them but also of that family at the Budapest cemetery, the young woman expecting a child, her parents who had come to the funeral of her husband—all sent to the other side, three generations killed together, the same day, the same hour. They had attended their own funeral. This is the essence of the tragedy of the Holocaust: three generations—the grandparents, the mother, and the unborn child—killed the same day.

I fell into a routine that varied little from one day to the next. The routine would have induced extreme boredom but for the knowledge that the possibility of death waited around every corner. Alertness to that possibility informed every waking minute.

Once in a while we would leave Camp E for another part of the camp to work for a few hours on little odd jobs, twenty or thirty boys at a time. I always took advantage of any chance to go. Sometimes we would get sod to put in front of the barrack to make it look nicer. The Nazis needed to mask the brutality of what they were doing, so that their surroundings would be more pleasant for them and they would not have to think about their actions. We had seen the cruelly ironic, now infamous line, "Arbeit Macht Frei"—"Work makes you free"—posted inside the barracks. Work made nobody free, but it did break the routine of otherwise formless days.

We also welcomed the opportunity to go to another camp because we could look for people we knew. Everywhere we went, we would ask, "Who are you? Where are you from?" It was very, very sad. We saw the Hungarian girls there, with their hair shorn. Some of the girls didn't even have barracks; they lived under the open sky.

We didn't want to attract attention to ourselves by doing anything that was active, so if there were no job to perform, we just hung about. We sat on the ground while the summer lasted, talking or daydreaming about how things used to be. I would pick up broken bits of brick and rub them together to make smooth geometric shapes. I don't know why the bricks were there, since the Germans did not want anything lying around that might be used as a weapon. But those small brick shards served as an important outlet for me; I carved small and beautiful shapes out of the rubble.

Survival was a goal that demanded vigilance and luck and I quickly learned that limited steps could be taken to help achieve it. I mastered several important survival techniques.

I knew I had to conserve my energy and not get sick. One important way to do that was to eat everything I could put my hands on. Food was the paramount concern. *Eat whatever they give you.* That is what my friend Sam told me. As prisoners, of course, we could only eat what they gave us. Some prisoners would steal from others and, if you didn't eat what you were given at once, the chances were strong that somebody would steal it. The food was terrible; not something that in any other circumstance would even be called food. But we were happy to have it—we only wished we had adequate amounts of it. I was lucky: I never even had a cold during my months at Auschwitz. I had dysentery at first, until my stomach adjusted to the water and the food.

We were given three meals a day. In the morning, after Appel, we were given a piece of bread with margarine and artificial coffee. Lunch was the main meal of the day. Prisoners from each barrack went to a central kitchen and returned with two large barrels of soup. Everybody had a metal bowl and a spoon. We lined up and each got a ladle of some sort of barley vegetable soup and a piece of dark German bread that must have had some nutritional value because it kept us going. As soon as we got our shares, we sat on the ground between the barracks and ate as fast as we could. At night, we got a slice of bread again, sometimes with margarine, occasionally with marmalade.

No matter what we were served, we were always hungry. Hunger, along with the threat of death, was a constant companion. Unabating, relentless, dogged hunger is an experience that is hard to comprehend and one that I, even after all these years, have not found a way to communicate.

My friends and I were lucky because our other Derecske friend, Sam Gluck who worked at the railroad where the trains came in, had access to food that had been brought by the incoming prisoners. Sam was courageous and practical and, from time to time when he could, he would throw food—bread or, now and then, sugar cubes—over the fifteen-foot high, electrified, barbed wire fence. That was an unbelievable treat.

These gifts from Sam put him in great danger since we were in the line of sight of the guards in the watch-towers. We were careful not to take food from anybody who could use it; what Sam gave us would have been thrown away or taken by the guards, or if there were enough of it, it would have been shipped back to Germany, as were the clothing and shoes.

Occasionally, the electricity on the fence was turned off and Sam could pass a bowl of food through the fence. Once, when we did this, a boy standing to my left was shot by one of the watch-tower guards. I heard a thud and a groan. I looked and saw a bullet hole in the boy's side. He walked away holding his hand over the wound. That was the last I saw of him. Could he have survived? I doubt it; he surely received no medical treatment. Had that bullet been intended for me? Possibly. There is no way to know; the Germans were completely random in their cruelties. While that was the only time I saw anybody shot, the sense of danger was constant. It was like combat. Any misstep could be fatal.

After food, staying away from physical violence was critical to survival. If you saw someone being mistreated, abused, or beaten, you could not interfere or help in any way. If you did, you would be beaten or worse. Once in a while, I saw an SS soldier stop a man and beat him. Often there was no apparent reason for it; the beatings were part of a pattern of psychological as well as physical intimidation. I was lucky: I was never physically beaten, though many were.

Staying out of trouble was another way to enhance your survival. If you got into trouble, you would get beaten. And, it was rare for anyone to recover from those injuries. Staying out of trouble to avoid physical punishment meant trying to be invisible. You couldn't conduct yourself in a manner that could be seen as provocative in any way. The guards demanded immediate and total submissive behavior. When the SS soldiers said, "Move," you moved. When they said, "Sit down," you sat down.

But I resisted in my mind and in my soul in order to remain myself, so as not to become an animal. At some point, Sam threw a prayer book containing the Psalms over the fence. During Appel, I stood in the last row and passed the time by reading the Psalms. I made myself race through them to see how fast I could do it. I did it many, many times. Reading the prayer book was an act of passive resistance, an assertion of self.

Another key to survival was holding on to some slight thread of individuality. I was able to do that through my friendships with Jack and Arthur whom I had known since I was four years old. In the midst of thousands, I was alone except for these two childhood friends. Having them with me was critical to my survival. Our bond of a common history was a tremendous source of strength for all three of us and provided the thread of individuality that we needed. Jack and Arthur were gutsy and smart. Of the three of us, Arthur could have passed for a German: he was tall and blond, with blue eyes.

The three of us were together to the very end. I believe the emotional support we gave each other was absolutely crucial to our survival. We were more than company for each other; it was us against them. The knowledge that we had lost everybody—the entire Derecske community—weighed heavily on us. We were determined to survive to tell the world what had happened. I do not know how to measure the psychological power of being there with hometown friends with whom I was so bonded, but I know that I would not have survived without them.

Our days were endless and we spent most of them doing absolutely nothing. While we were terribly homesick, we were together and talked endlessly about life at home. Uppermost in our minds was one question: were we ever going to be home again with whoever was left of our families? Being interminably hungry, I thought of food: my mother's wonderful bread, the magical Sabbath table that transformed a simple meal into a festive experience. Would we ever sit around a Sabbath table again? The memory of it, the hope that one day it would be possible again, kept me going. I had to believe that my return to that time was possible.

Finally, refusing to give up was essential. Giving up was the first step in one's destruction. I saw youngsters who had given up. I saw in their eyes that they had lost hope. I saw the despair in their shuffling walk, in the fact that they stopped washing. Starvation produces a kind of puffiness around the eyes that can be spotted easily. When I saw it, I knew they would not last long.

Adaptation to life in the camps was partly a matter of chance and luck, but also depended on things like age, social, cultural, even class background. People who came from less privileged backgrounds had a better chance to survive because they were sturdier, already accustomed to coping in physically challenging environments, to making do with less. Perhaps they were even stronger because they had been obliged to do more physical work in normal circumstances. Some of us who survived had arrived at Auschwitz already physically tough and were better prepared. I think it was for that reason that some of our finest people, people who were more refined, more cultured, perished.

Every few days somebody died. They died from brutal treatment, from malnutrition, from exhaustion, or depression. Many simply gave in to hopelessness and despair. When someone died, prisoners would carry the body outside and lay it on the ground. Before too long, a special work detail of prisoners would take the dead bodies to the crematorium.

Some privileged adult prisoners who had been in the camp for three or four years, who had become part of the prison infrastructure, were allowed greater freedom of movement: they could move around without work details. They were, comparatively speaking, well fed. They could even have a kind of gathering in the room of a barrack leader.

We saw Czech prisoners who had been in Auschwitz for three years, who looked strong and well-nourished. They lived in a separate area called Canada. Of course, many of them were killed because they knew too much, for example, that the gold and the clothes taken from prisoners, even their hair, had been sent to Germany. But these "privileged" prisoners were always replaced with others. I don't know why they didn't just go on strike and say no, we are not going to do anything. The Germans couldn't do all the work themselves. They knew they were working for the enemy, but they had no choice. They were slaves like all of us.

This is a tragedy of the human condition: people can be made to behave in ways that they never would if their own survival were not at stake.

A heroic act of rebellion occurred at Auschwitz-Birkenau in October 1944, though at the time I didn't know what was happening. The *sondercommandos*, the prisoners who worked in the crematoria, learned that they were to be gassed. They were eye-witnesses to the slaughter and could not be allowed to survive. The sondercommandos received special treatment, particularly better food, in return for the work they did in the gas chambers and crematoria. At that late stage in the war, fewer new shipments of Jews arrived at the camp—there were, after all, few left to capture—so the need for the services of the sondercommandos was declining.

About two hundred had been killed at the end of September. So, when the SS guards came to take away another three hundred, the sondercommandos decided not to cooperate in their executions. They attacked the SS guards with whatever tools they could get their hands on, hammers, axes or stones. A few guards were killed. One crematorium was blown up by dynamite that had been smuggled into the camp by women who worked outside the camp. After the uprising the women were caught and shot. The men broke through the fences and escaped into the woods. Some paused on the way to cut the wires to a women's camp so that they too might escape.

But nobody escaped and survived. Some made their way to a nearby village where the Germans surrounded them in a barn. They set the barn on fire, burning to death everyone who was inside. Others were shot in the woods. About two hundred and fifty people were killed that day. Our camps were immediately locked down and all prisoners locked inside their barracks. If the sondercommandos had been able to destroy three or four of the crematoria a few months earlier, then Hungarian Jewry might have been saved. Regardless of its outcome, the rebellion was an act of true heroism.

Throughout my time at Auschwitz-Birkenau, "selections" were held to choose individuals to be killed in the gas chambers.

We lived in constant fear of these selections.

We never knew from day to day if there would be one or who would be chosen. The SS would come and count the prisoners as usual, but sometimes, without warning or pattern, a committee would come as well. A prisoner would be pulled out, apparently at random. Perhaps he looked sick or had somehow unfavorably attracted the attention of one of the guards.

Arthur, Jack and I gradually became more knowledgeable about the selections and the manner in which they were implemented from Sam who knew more than we did. One day he warned us, "I heard there is going to be a selection on the left side of the camp tomorrow night, so be careful." We asked two boys on the right side, two tall boys who would not be chosen because of their obvious health, for help. (Arthur was tall and didn't need a stand-in.) We said, "Stand in for us, for in Block 11, what counts is the number of prisoners, not who they are." It was very important to us that we not endanger anybody else, and we didn't because there was no required quota. The two substitutes may have saved our lives that day. After the Appel, we returned to our barracks. We only did this once.

After a while, we no longer benefited from warnings from Sam; he was transferred to work in Germany, eventually ending up at Buchenwald, where he was reunited with his father who had earlier been conscripted into the labor battalions. For me, the most dramatic moment, my closest brush with death, came on Erev Yom Kippur, the day before the Day of Atonement, 1944. Word spread that the Nazis wanted five thousand potato pickers, though it was late in the season. Deportations from the ghettos had ceased and the transports weren't coming any more. My friends and I thought that maybe the war was going to end and the Nazis had little need for manpower. Though we didn't understand it at the time, the need for manpower was actually growing more and more desperate. At that point in the war, Hitler had no thought of surrender and the German command was ready to press any human who could still function into service for the war effort.

Birkenau was divided into sections separated by electrified barbed wire. Each section was in the shape of a large rectangle, barracks on both sides with a wide road between them. At the end of camp E was a soccer field with a goal post. Perhaps the guards played soccer there, although I don't remember ever seeing it. On the vertical of the goal post they nailed a cross bar to measure the height of the prisoners; we had to strip to the waist, walk under the goal post and stand under the cross bar. An SS officer stood in front of it to examine each person one at a time. If you were tall enough, you lived.

The column on the right side was made up of the boys who were tall enough and seemed strong enough to pass the guard's inspection. If he sent you across the way to the other side, it meant disaster. It was psychological torture; I think they had made up their minds to destroy half the camp that night.

Arthur, who was tall, passed the inspection but Jack and I did not. We were told to stand on the edge of the road on the left, separated from the stronger boys. Our working rule of thumb was that it was never safe to be put into the group that looked less healthy. Jack realized we were in danger and watched the SS officer who walked up and down the road to keep the groups apart. The guard, with his back to us, bent over to tie his shoe. Jack whispered, "Let's get out of here," so we sneaked across the road into the heart of the column of stronger boys. Some were angry with us for coming to their side but we did not endanger anybody since the SS did not count the boys. Once among the stronger boys, we were safe — at least for the moment.

Among those we left behind, those sent to die, were two boys we had known all our lives. That afternoon we lost the son of our Hebrew teacher, whose name was Fiuka Sternberger, and we lost Sandor Spitz, with whom I had walked to school every day. He was an only child. In Derecske, his mother, afraid her son would catch cold, would come out of the house and remind him on bitter cold days to put on his scarf and gloves and button his coat. That's all I could think about that day: how his mother used to worry about him catching cold. Now he was heading for the gas chamber. He was sixteen years old.

Jack, Arthur and I lived through that night. There was a universal lockdown, the weak and the strong in separate barracks. That night was long and we didn't get much sleep. We never went back to Block 11 again.

The following morning the ones chosen for the gas chamber broke out and ran all over the camp. There was an immediate lockdown again, and the SS guards rounded up those who had escaped, hunting them mercilessly. The boys hid wherever they could. Some of them crawled inside a pile of rectangular wooden frames stacked together on one side of the empty field but they were caught.

Two days later they were all killed.

This was the last selection. The last time. If it hadn't been for that last selection, perhaps many of the boys would have survived like I did.

They were either too short.

Or too young.

What happened to them was the most extreme cruelty.

That was the essence of Auschwitz-Birkenau. Thousands were killed in that episode.

Five thousand teenage boys.

The day after the selection was Yom Kippur. We were let out of the barracks as usual but there was no roll call. There was an eerie quiet all over camp. Jack, Arthur, and I, and several others, by a kind of common impulse entered an empty barrack. We went to the corner furthest from the door and began to recite the morning prayer. We mostly knew the prayers by heart. We prayed from memory whatever we could recall. It was instinctive, part of our nature and culture from childhood. A symbol of the remaining spark of humanity left to us. Though we were prisoners, our thoughts were free.

Chapter Eight

After

Life in the camp returned to its previous "normal" until the beginning of November, when the Nazis needed to assemble a transport of mechanics to work in Germany. The German industrialists, including IG Farben who had built a major chemical industry near Auschwitz, used slave labor as did many German companies and companies in all the German-occupied countries. The German situation was desperate and workers were needed in all industries— farming, mining, and factory work.

The guards told us that the Bussing-NAG company, a truck manufacturer, had requested one thousand workers from Auschwitz who were still fit for labor. They first looked for metal workers, but by the time we were selected, having a body strong enough for manual labor was the only real criterion. I believe I was in the third of the three transports, comprised of Poles, Hungarians, Czechs, and Slovaks. Most of the earlier transports had been Poles from the Lodz ghetto.

My spirits lifted because I knew I would have a better chance for survival if I were at a work camp than if I were to remain in Auschwitz. Jack, Arthur and I passed ourselves off as mechanics and were chosen for the work detail.

We left Auschwitz-Birkenau on November 11th, 1944, a Saturday night. I had been there for 119 days.

Snow fell lightly as we walked to the railroad track along the road between the barbed wire fences that separated the major camps. We began to march out of Camp E toward the railroad ramp.

I asked Jack, "Are the train doors open?" The SS always lied to us. It was possible they were taking us to the other side of the train to the gas chambers. We never could be sure.

He answered, "Yes."

The guards herded us onto the train, a long line of boxcars, and the doors shut and locked. After a short while, the train pulled away. I remember the jubilation, the tremendous elation I felt. I didn't feel the intense anxiety I had felt on the train trip to Auschwitz. This time I only felt curiosity about our destination. This, I dared hope, was the beginning of the end. My friends and I had achieved a major, but still penultimate victory—while we weren't yet free, we were leaving Auschwitz-Birkenau alive. We felt triumphant.

The cold was bitter on the train and my right foot became frostbitten. The pain was terrible, one I had never before experienced. A kind man on the train, about my father's age, comforted me, advising, "Don't step on it; don't touch it." A few weeks later in Braunschweig, this kind man died during a work detail clearing out a bombed-out building when a wall fell on him. I do not know his name, but I remember him and his kindness.

After the war, I learned that many prisoners had been force-marched to Germany from Auschwitz. Many died along the road from exhaustion. I paid a small price for the train ride: frostbitten toes on my right foot.

The cold lasted the entire trip; perhaps the warmth from our bodies packed so tightly together kept us alive. Occasionally we were given some bread and, from time to time, the guards would unlock the boxcar and allow us to walk around during long waits in hidden parts of railroad yards. Once I found a pile of frozen potato peels along the side of the rails; I happily filled my pockets and shared them with Jack and Arthur.

After a week or so, we arrived in Braunschweig, Germany to work at the Bussing-NAG factory. While we were not free, we thought freedom was near and we had greater confidence that we would survive.

Braunschweig was an industrial center that was also famous for its sausage, "Braunschweiger wurst," though of course we saw none of it. We lived in a small camp near the city's railroad station with only three or four barracks and a makeshift clinic for those who were ill. Our camp was one of several housing prisoners, primarily Poles, Russians and Frenchmen. The barracks were just as overcrowded as they had been at Auschwitz, and the stench was so foul that the guards rarely came inside.

The workers at the factory included men and boys, fewer than a thousand in all. Many were boys roughly my age; very few were younger. We were scared when we first arrived because when the inspection team from the factory came, the Germans looked us over and said, "What have they sent us, the kindergarten?" We were afraid they would send us back to Auschwitz-Birkenau, which would have meant death, but their need for any kind of labor helped us to survive.

Our daily routine started before dawn. For breakfast, we were given a slice of bread and a mug of what they called coffee. We lined up to be counted. The guard who roused us at 4 A.M. was a criminal and an anti-Semite. He taunted us, saying things like, "You're not going to get any roast duck here. I know what you like, the roast chicken, the goose liver, but you won't get it here. None of that stuff here."

The winter of 1945 was a bitter one and, like the soldiers in the Battle of the Bulge, we suffered from the harsh cold and tremendous blizzards. By six o'clock in the morning, we were at the factory. Most of the time we were driven the mile to the factory in a military truck, but sometimes we marched on the hard cobblestone streets through an old section of the city. Some sections were completely bombed out, a wasteland, but others had been untouched and were charming. As I marched, I wondered if I would ever walk on a sidewalk again. We went five in a rank, guarded by soldiers. To this day, I still think of walking on a sidewalk as a metaphor for freedom. Our enslavement was so severe that even walking on a sidewalk was an unattainable dream.

Some of the boys worked indoors, where they could stay warm, performing semi-skilled tasks in relatively clean surroundings. I was not that lucky. I worked as part of an outdoor crew as a handyman. I sanded the driveway when vehicles were to be moved and I lugged steel bars from one place to another. Sometimes I had to carry buckets of cement up two or three flights of stairs where bomb-damaged parts of the factory were being restored. To have done that for a long time would have killed me; one cannot carry buckets of cement all day on the kind of diet we had.

In the yard, a steel barrel was occasionally used to burn scraps of wood. We warmed ourselves by it whenever we could. The truck used to drive us to the factory was fueled by coal, equipped with some sort of gasification device. There was a big cylinder mounted on the rear of the driver's cabin that held the coal. Sometimes we had to wait for the fire to get hot before the truck would move. It was the first time I had ever seen anything like that.

Since the factory was closed on Sunday, we had a day off from the factory work. Nonetheless, they roused us at four A.M. and made us stand outside. Sometimes we were put to work moving garbage from one place to another; I couldn't imagine a purpose to it other than to keep us busy. But they may have been doing us a favor because we were in the fresh air, moving and getting exercise. Maybe exercise was the point—that was another of the strange paradoxical obsessions that the Germans had: they wanted to keep us healthy so that we could walk to our death.

The death rate at Braunschweig was high from the start. We were starving when we arrived and the heavy work took its toll. Men died every day. They would drop from exhaustion or die from chronic diarrhea or fevers. Dead bodies were stacked up in one of the barracks and, about once a week, a truck would load them up and take them away.

We no longer wore the black and white prison uniforms. We had been given warmer clothes before we left Auschwitz-Birkenau. We had been allowed to get clothing from a warehouse barrack that had been used to store things people had brought with them from home. The fact that we had somewhat better clothes probably saved our lives. I found normal pants and a jacket, shoes, one pair of socks, one shirt, and one pair of underwear.

The clothes were clean when we got them, but we had no way to wash them or ourselves so, in Braunschweig, garment lice became a constant problem. Once you got infected with them, they were impossible to get rid of. You would sit down at night and pick them out of your shirt and kill them, but you could never find them all. There was a cast iron coal-fired stove in the barracks, so we would take off our shirts and pass them over the red-hot stove and hear the lice crackle. Delousing ourselves was a constant job; we never really won the fight against them, but we kept them enough at bay that we prevented a typhus outbreak. That, in and of itself, was a victory.

Finding sufficient food was still a constant struggle. We were given bread and occasionally a white vegetable, maybe a turnip. Potatoes were scarce, though sometimes we would find a piece of potato in our soup. Potatoes were the food staple of Europe, but they were not about to give them to us. We had a thirty-minute break in the middle of the day for our soup and we ate as fast as we could. If we were at the end of the line to be fed and didn't have time to eat before the break was over, the guards would knock our bowls out of our hands.

One day in the early spring we came back to the camp from the factory to find a farmer's cart outside the gate, a cart filled with carrots. The officer at the head of the column said, "This is for you, take it." We filled our pockets with as many carrots as we could and ate them for days.

While at Braunschweig, one of the block elders was a brutal German prisoner, a foreman who had been a boxer, a man who took great delight in hitting the prisoners, especially large, strong men. Once I saw him hit one man with his fist and the man fell like a log. I was never physically abused by the SS, but I was once given a couple of shellackings by a capo who happened to be in a bad mood. Even a prisoner could beat you up.

The railroad station was often bombed at night and, while the sounds of the explosions were tremendous, we paid no attention. Most nights, I fell asleep to the encouraging sound of sirens and bombs. We weren't allowed to leave the barracks, so I turned over and went back to sleep. If a bomb hit the barracks I would be killed: there was nothing I could do about it.

One afternoon in the late spring, I remember lying on a field watching the Allied planes go by. They flew in groups of five. *Five, ten, fifteen, twenty*, I counted, finally stopping at one hundred.

Soon afterward, in the middle of March, our camp was evacuated. We marched for the better part of a day to our next destination, the camp Watenstedt. The fact that we had eaten those carrots for a couple of weeks gave us extra energy to make the march. I assign magical powers to those carrots. A huge steel plant, the Hermann Goering Works, was located near Watenstedt, a camp that held French, Russian, and Italian prisoners of war.

I surmise now that we had been evacuated from Braunschweig because the Germans intended to destroy the camp. They were concentrating their prisoners in fewer places, for eventual liquidation.

One day, they took all our clothes away. For an eerie twenty-four hours, we had no clothes at all. We were deloused and walked around in blankets, nothing more. We worried about not getting our clothes back, but after a few days we did. During that time, we had to sleep naked. One night, while Jack and I slept together for warmth, somebody stole the blanket off our bunk and disappeared into the dark with it. Jack and I crept along the row of bunks looking for someone who was asleep deeply enough so that we could take his blanket. We knew if he awoke cold, he would do the same. After everything we had endured, we were not going to freeze to death. That was the only time we acted like that.

About this time in April, a gigantic air raid took place at the Hermann Goering Works adjacent to the camp. I literally had to run for my life. I looked at the sky and listened for the whistle of the bomb coming down and ran the other way. Somehow, I took it in stride; it was par for the course. Surrounded by danger, I watched the guards in their towers fire their machine guns at the low-flying planes. This was near the end of the war, and the British and U.S. air forces were softening up the territory for the advancing armies. Demoralizing the German population was also part of their plan.

We only stayed a few weeks at Watenstedt. From there, we were taken by train to Ravensbruck, another concentration camp that, prior to our arrival, had held Russian, French and Italian prisoners of war. With every move we did not know whether we were going to be killed or put to work. Conditions on the train were appalling: we were jammed together and almost everyone was sick. Many had diarrhea and, of course, there were no facilities for relief. Many died on the train; there was at least one stop made to take off the dead bodies.

While at Ravensbruck, my right foot became infected, an aftereffect of the frostbite and I couldn't walk on it. With my horrible infection and crippled condition, I thought to myself, "Oh my God, this is the end." I saw some so-called doctors taking sick calls in the yard, but I didn't want to go to them. There was no knowing whether one would get treatment or be shot. One morning, when I got out of my bunk bed I stepped on my right foot and the infection exploded, pus gushing out. I casually walked over to the faucet at the latrine at the end of the barrack. I rinsed off my foot, tore away a piece of my shirt, and wrapped my foot in it. A few days later it was healed. I was amazed because I believed I was close to death at the time. Gangrene could have set in or blood poisoning. So many people died just from being worn out; an actual infection was almost always fatal. I was fortunate that the infection was localized. I hadn't wanted them to amputate my foot and was lucky that it healed by itself.

Something fantastic happened in Ravensbruck. Soon after we arrived, we received American Red Cross packages that were probably intended for American POWs. The food was too rich for our stomachs and we got sick from what we ate—tremendous diarrhea and dysentery. Still, the chocolate and cookies and crackers seemed heaven-sent. A POW came up to me and grabbed my package of food out of my hand. Whatever was in the box and not in my pocket was taken. I cried bitterly over the loss of a few crackers and cookies.

Then, a surprise. One Saturday night they called for all the Jewish men to assemble. That could be good or it could be very, very bad; we didn't know. We assembled and stood to be counted. Then we were sent to bed. The following morning we were told, "All of you Jews who were counted last night assemble outside." They marched us to the railroad siding. There we were again given fresh Red Cross packages and then we climbed up into yet another freight train.

It was a gorgeous mid-April, spring day. Unlike previous train travel, this time the box-car doors were unlocked and open. Since the guards were not harassing us and we could feel the fresh air through the open doors, we were in a great mood. Unbelievable rumors flew that we were going to Denmark to be released. Upon the encouragement of one of the guards, I remember singing a Hungarian song. Yet, a few of the Polish kids didn't like that and gave me a tongue lashing, saying that I was a *quisling*—a traitor—which made me furious.

The trip to Denmark should have taken only a few days. But for whatever reason we didn't get there—it was said that a strategic bridge somewhere had been bombed and destroyed. Our dejection was overwhelming. We were on that train for a week, going back and forth, back and forth. It seemed as though the SS didn't know where to take us, what to do with us.

One frightening night, our train was machine gunned by an Allied aircraft. We were almost killed by our friends. They of course didn't know; as far as they could tell, our train could have been full of enemy troops. Years later, when I watched newsreels from the war and saw how the fighter bombers used to strafe the trains, I thought, "My God, that was a train I might have been on."

After a week on the train, they dropped us at our final camp, called Wobbelin, near Ludwigslust, in the middle of a forest. It was late April 1945. We arrived totally exhausted. Wobbelin, known as "horrible Wobbelin," a sub-camp of Neuengamme, existed for only ten weeks. Many came, as we did, as inmates from factories and labor camps. Its population was mixed: there were French, Belgian, and East European prisoners, all suffering terribly from brutality and starvation. Jews were probably in the minority there.

Wobbelin was not an extermination camp as such—it did not have gas chambers and crematoria—but it was a death camp anyway. Everyone who came there was already weak and often sick. Many simply starved to death there in those ten weeks. Conditions were so appalling that people died by the hundreds from hunger, dysentery and other maladies. Bodies piled up unattended. Finally they would be trucked away to mass graves.

I remember with particular horror the French and Belgian POWs, who were crazy from starvation. Even going to the bathroom was dangerous; if they saw that you had a cigarette, they would kill you for it. Somebody came back from the latrine and reported that he had seen an act of cannibalism. I was sickened. I don't remember if I ever actually went into the bathroom there. The prison capos had the presence of mind—and maybe the humanity—to say, "Give us the rest of your Red Cross packages." They knew the Russian POWs would kill us for any food we had. They confiscated our packages except for what we could put in our pockets. Nonetheless, the food was still too rich for us and anyone who ate it became quite ill.

The physical arrangement at Wobbelin was worse than in the other camps. The barracks were long, low buildings with tiers of racks to serve for beds. There was no water for washing. The only water I remember was a pump in a yard between two of the buildings. One building was called an infirmary, but it was simply a place to die. When liberation came, the soldiers found it stacked high with emaciated corpses.

Arthur, Jack and I were at Wobbelin for fewer than ten days. On the night of May 1st, we were ordered to climb into open coal cars on the railroad siding at the camp. I didn't know what the SS intended to do with us. While standing in the train throughout the night, we discussed what might happen to us. Maybe the Nazis had lost their nerve. Maybe the Allied troops were too close. Maybe they thought an airplane would strafe us. Would they machine gun us in those cars?

In the morning, the guards screamed, "Out, out! Back to camp!" We were supposed to line up as we had done so many times in the past. But this time nobody lined up. An unconscious sense of something new permeated the air. The SS guards had lost their authority or simply no longer cared. We walked back in a disorganized fashion, all discipline gone. The SS let us be.

Back at the camp, I lay down on the ground and went to sleep. Some time later I heard a loud noise and woke to a gorgeous sunny day, brilliant blue skies over my head. It was May 2nd, 1945. Jack stood over me and yelled, "They broke down the gates; the SS ran away."

I replied, "Aah, I'm tired; let me sleep." But Jack insisted I wake up.

When I did wake up, we looked at each other, realizing the enormity of the moment. We immediately began shouting, "It's over! It's over! I can't believe it's over!" I felt joyously triumphant that I had survived against all the odds.

At mid-morning, an American jeep with two soldiers, one very tall and one shorter, entered the camp. When they got out of the jeep, a few prisoners picked up one of the soldiers and threw him in the air, calling him "Texas, Texas, Texas." We knew they were Americans. One of us spoke English and learned that these soldiers were on patrol and had discovered us by accident. The troops were to come later in the afternoon.

In between the time the patrolling soldiers came and the main troops arrived, prisoners had broken down the fence and left the confines of the camp fences. Jack, Arthur and I found some food stored on a nearby train. Just an hour earlier, the crazed, starved Belgian, French and Dutch POWs could have killed us but now we were like one big brotherhood of freed men. Everybody had food. We made fires and cooked potatoes. May 2nd was one beautiful, beautiful day.

Later that afternoon, the U.S. troops arrived, like liberating angels. It was an advance party that evidently had been staffed with men who spoke European languages. One of the soldiers gave me a thick chocolate bar, but I couldn't keep anything like that down in my stomach.

Some spoke Yiddish; they cried when we told them what had happened to us. However, there was little conversation among us. Their very presence spoke for us more than words.

I have never been and will never be as happy as I was on that day.

I have never and will never again experience the feeling of transcendent jubilation I felt on that day.

Life could never be bad again. Whatever would happen to us from then on could only be good. Everyone was excited; we jumped up and down with elation. Our joy was irrepressible.

But many prisoners were too weak and exhausted from starvation to rejoice. Men lay dead or dying everywhere, too far gone in their misery to be aware of freedom.

Arthur, Jack and I had achieved an enormous victory.

We had outlived Hitler.

The war was over!

We–I–had survived the Nazis.

Chapter Nine

Toward Recovery

After a few days, the GIs took us into the city and placed us in an abandoned public building where we slept on the floor on piles of straw. Jack, Arthur and I were quite ill, coughing so badly we thought we had the flu or pneumonia. Nonetheless, on Friday, we decided to make a Shabbat dinner. We went into the courtyard of a quadrangle of public buildings where there was an American military kitchen. We had powdered chicken soup from the army kitchen; Jack's job was to find meat, I was to find bread and milk, and Arthur a cooking pot. I came upon a German canteen, a big soldiers' canteen. I saw a store with a long line of people outside, went to the head of the line, entered, smacked my container on the counter, and demanded that it be filled to the brim. He answered that he didn't have enough milk. I shouted in broken German, "Yes, you do; give me all the milk I didn't have last year. And you'd better fill it up or I'll go get the Military Police." So he filled it up. I was no longer timid, but gutsy and cunning.

The canteen filled with milk was too heavy for me to carry. I had had the strength to ask for it, but not to carry it. I sat down on the steps leading up to a public building. As I rested, a young GI came by on a bike, a peach-fuzz kid no more than nineteen years old. He signaled to me to wait, then came back with a big loaf of fresh white bread. He took my milk and walked with me back to the building where we were staying.

Jack had found that the French POWs had shot a horse, so there was meat. And Arthur had found a big pot. We had an open fire outside and sliced up the meat. We put the dried chicken soup in water and put the meat in. So we had Shabbat—white bread for the challah and chicken soup made with horse-meat. But we were still sick and couldn't keep anything down.

Soon, the Allies established their separate jurisdictions in Germany—British, French, Russian, and American zones—and Jack, Arthur and I were moved to a hospital in Luneburg in the British zone. All three of us were put into one room. An American military doctor told the nurses, "Anything these boys want, whenever they want it, you'd better give it to them."

Our recovery had begun.

I learned years later from Chaplain George B. Woods of the 82nd Airborne Division that the Americans who liberated the camp were so horrified by what they found that they were determined to show the local people what had been happening around them. Nobody, of course, professed to know anything. No one in the German army surrounding the area had been willing to indicate an awareness of what happened inside the camp. Several army chaplains who had taken refuge in a local monastery were incredulous when told about the atrocities. Wobbelin was visible from the main road. The local residents must have known.

Under the leadership of Major General Gavin, commander of the 82nd Airborne Division, local residents were compelled to walk through the camp and the infirmary, in particular, to see the piles of corpses and to experience the stench and the filth. They did so with reluctance; some were in tears when they came out, but many were stone-faced.

Later, when mass graves were discovered, the Allies made the townspeople dig up the bodies and transport them to a new cemetery created in front of the palace of the Duke of Mecklenburg in Ludwigslust, where they were re-buried in individual graves. To give the dead a decent burial, the Americans made sure that every grave was six feet deep. When the graves were prepared in long rows and the corpses laid beside them, the captured army officers and the townspeople were required to walk along the corridor between the graves and look at the bodies. General Gavin, the youngest major general in the American army, was determined that the German civilians see with their own eyes the horrors that had surrounded them. He wanted to make sure they would remember the horror for the rest of their lives. He could not compel the whole German nation to see, but he could make sure that the people of Ludwigslust did. Many of the Nazi army officers would only look straight ahead, as though they were unaware—or indifferent to—what they saw around them.

On May 7, 1945, a memorial service was held by the Americans. Chaplain Major George B. Woods of the 82nd Airborne Division, spoke to the assembled townspeople. Standing beside the two hundred grave-sites, the GIs, the German officers and civilians, Major Woods gave this eulogy:

We are assembled here today before God and in the sight of man to give a proper and reverent burial to the victims of atrocities committed by armed forces in the name of and by the order of the German Government. These 200 bodies were found by the American army in a concentration camp 4 miles north of the city of Ludwigslust.

The crimes here committed in the name of the German people and by their acquiescence were minor compared to those to be found in concentration camps elsewhere in Germany. Here there were no gas chambers, no crematories; these men of Holland, Russia, Poland, Czechoslovakia, and France were simply allowed to starve to death. Within four miles of your comfortable homes, 4,000 men were forced to live like animals, deprived even of the food you would give to your dogs. In three weeks, 1,000 of these men were starved to death; 800 of them were buried in pits in the nearby woods. These 200 who lie before us in these graves were found piled four and five feet high in one building and with the sick and dying in other buildings.

The world has long been horrified at the crimes of the German nation; these crimes were never clearly brought to light until the armies of the United Nations overran Germany. This is not war conducted by the international rules of warfare. This is murder such as is not even known among savages.

Though you claim no knowledge of these acts, you are still individually and collectively responsible for these atrocities, for they were committed by a government elected to office by yourselves in 1933 and continued in office by your indifference to organized brutality. It should be the first resolve of the German people that never again should any leader or party bring them to such moral degradation as is exhibited here.

It is the custom of the United States Army through its Chaplain's Corps to insure a proper and decent burial to any deceased person whether he be civilian, or soldier, friend, or foe, according to religious preference. The Supreme Commander of the Allied Forces has ordered that all atrocity victims be buried in a public place, and that the cemetery be given the same perpetual care that is given to all military cemeteries. Crosses will be placed at the heads of the graves; a stone monument will be set up in memory of these deceased. Protestant, Catholic, and Jewish prayers will be said by Chaplains Wood, Hannan, and Wall of the 82nd Airborne Division for these victims as we lay them to rest and commit them into the hands of our Heavenly Father in the hope that the world will not again be faced with such barbarity.

From the hospital in Luneburg, we watched the British troops marching in parade. We stayed in Luneburg until July 15th in order to recover our capacity to eat and regain some strength. Jack, Arthur, and I recovered rapidly in the makeshift hospital. At first we were put on a special diet of light food, things like oatmeal and farina. We ate little or no meat at first. We were in the care of doctors from the Allied military forces, but the nurses were German. Jack, Arthur, and I shared a small room, formerly an office, with two other boys. We were separated from adult patients, who were either French or Italian, who had also just been liberated and were recovering from malnutrition and other related problems from their internment. After a few weeks we were able to eat normal food and we began to look like normal human beings again.

Once we were well enough, we were allowed to explore the city. Luneburg was a neat and clean medium-sized city. It was a pleasure to walk along the streets. There was no question of buying anything, since we had no money, and there was little in the shops, but I was overjoyed simply to walk on the sidewalks again and relished being a free man.

One day, as I walked on the street with a former prisoner, we saw a British soldier light a cigarette, take three puffs, and throw it away. The man said, "Do you see why the Allies won the war?"

"Why?" I asked.

He answered, "They can throw away three-quarters of a cigarette." If an average soldier could afford to throw away three-quarters of a cigarette, then I began to imagine the depth of resources and supplies the Allied armies must have had. He picked up the cigarette, held it, and exclaimed, "This is why the Allies won the war."

In early July, we learned that the Swedish government had invited former prisoners to go to Sweden as guests of the Swedish people. We were told schools would be set up for us and we would get a monthly allowance. My friends and I debated whether we should accept the invitation or return to Hungary first. The motivation for returning to Hungary was simple enough: we wanted to know who else survived. We thought that if we returned home we would finally know.

Even though we knew little about Sweden, the invitation was enticing. We thought we could return to Hungary later if we wanted to so we decided to accept the offer and explore the new opportunities offered in the Land of the Midnight Sun. At the very least, it would be a wonderful experience to be in a country untouched by the horrors of war. By that time, Auschwitz felt very far behind me.

With other young people, we went first by train to Bergen-Belsen, a former concentration camp that had been turned into a giant transit center for displaced persons and remained so for several years. We were housed in several red brick, high-rise buildings that had been used by the German military and the camp administration. The British army burned the barracks where the inmates had been imprisoned as a public health measure. Like the other survivors who passed through, we wrote our names in the big registration book in the central office. Quite by accident, we met several women from home who said they had seen my sisters, Ilona and Iren. We found their names in the registry and discovered that they had passed through Bergen-Belsen and returned to Hungary just a few days before we came. I was thrilled to discover that at least two other members of my family had survived. I wondered how soon we would meet. It was no surprise, of course, that we didn't meet there; the level of confusion was enormous.

Jack and Arthur, however, did not learn of the survival of their relatives for several more months. By this point, our three-way friendship was quite powerful; the experiences we shared and survived bound us forever. Though we were not technically family, perhaps our bond was even closer than family.

A few days later, we departed by train to the port city of Lubeck, Germany on the North Sea. From there, we embarked on a white ship sailing to Sweden. Before disembarking the following morning, we were requested to provide information concerning our country of birth, date of birth, and names of family members. Except for my Bar Mitzvah, my family had never celebrated my birthday and I wasn't sure of the precise date. I knew the year of my birth—1928—and the month—February—but I was not sure of the day. I remember my parents saying that the year of my birth was a leap year. I decided then that I must have been born on February 29. Years later, I obtained an official birth certificate from Hungary. I opened the envelope and looked at the certificate, hoping that my guess had been right. According to the certificate, my birthday was February 9, 1928. I had lost my birthday. I decided to keep the 29th as my new birthday. I believed I had earned a new birthday for my new life.

Chapter Ten

Rebirth

Our ship pulled into the harbor at Halsingborg, Sweden on July 18, 1945, a glorious summer day. The city was a vision from a dream, untouched by the war, bathed in golden summer light. Its streets were immaculate, its parks carefully tended and landscaped with red and white geraniums and red begonias. The low buildings were white or pastel, with roofs of red tile. The city was human in scale and welcoming in appearance. The atmosphere conveyed a sense of peace and the fundamental goodness of life. I was powerfully struck by the sight of people relaxing on park benches, strolling along the waterways, enjoying the serenity and the summer sun. Children riding bicycles, old men smoking their pipes. Truly, it was heaven to boys who, only an overnight boat-ride before, had emerged from the wartime desolation of burned-out, bombed-out cities.

This world was new, a world where kindness was a governing value. Only a few months earlier, I had been a candidate for annihilation. In Sweden, I was warmly welcomed as a cherished human being. This experience had an unforgettable impact on me, renewing my faith in the power of human kindness. That faith has never left me.

Our welcome, while friendly, was necessarily somewhat institutional. To make sure that we had no diseases that could be passed along to the Swedes, we were quarantined for the first week. Initially, we were housed in a residential neighborhood in a multi-story school building that had been converted into a small hotel. Altogether, we were fewer than two hundred people — teenagers and adults of both sexes. Men and women occupied different floors in the same building. Accommodations were basic but clean, much like a boarding school. We slept in two-level bunk beds, but there were mattresses, sheets and pillows, and, coming as we had from the war, it was luxurious.

We spent our days outside, gazing across the fence at the people who came to look at us. These Nordic people, mostly tall and blond, seemed fascinated by our different appearance. They stood for hours at the chain link fence that surrounded the school, sometimes passing us candies through the fence.

One night, there was an outdoor talent show. When I learned about it, I volunteered to sing. Hundreds of Swedes gathered to listen. I sang *La Paloma*, a ballad popular in Hungary and all over Europe. The following day many visitors called me to the fence, looking for the Hungarian boy who had sung the night before. I received enough candy to last the rest of the summer. What a welcome! I was overwhelmed by the outpouring of kindness.

After a few weeks, we were allowed to explore the city. We received either coupons or cash to buy new clothes and before long we had entirely new wardrobes. One of my great pleasures was the purchase of a double-breasted gray suit, one blue dress shirt, one red necktie, and one pair of dress shoes. I jokingly referred to these clothes as *the* suit, *the* shirt, and *the* necktie. Owning new clothes was a luxury beyond belief and I felt perfectly equipped for my new life as a well-dressed young man.

A new life in a new world restored our individuality. At the age of seventeen, I was looking into the future with great exuberance.

As part of an overall plan for Jewish orphans brought to Sweden, the Swedish authorities created special schools across the country. From Halsingborg, Arthur, Jack, and I were transferred to Avesta, a summer camp in the central part of Sweden, in the middle of a deep forest adjoining a large lake. We spent the rest of the summer of 1945 there. Rowing on the lake was a wonderful new experience for me. The stay at Avesta was made very pleasant through the efforts of the camp's director. I communicated with her, using a few words of Swedish, a little German, and lots of hand signals. One day, a group of us, boys and girls, went to a movie; we noticed that teenagers at the movie were wearing windbreakers that we thought very snazzy. All of us wanted those windbreakers. A group of boys went to the director's office and made an impassioned plea for windbreakers. She smiled at us, picked up the telephone, and called some official to authorize buying them. Within a week, we had windbreakers. It did not take much to make us happy.

There was a moment at Avesta summer camp when my path might have taken a different turn. When visitors came, children who had some kind of talent were asked to perform; I was often asked to sing. A rich Swedish family who were steel manufacturers had come to tea and asked me to sing two Hungarian folk songs. The guests were so taken with my songs they offered to adopt me. I was of course much flattered but refused—I decided that I had not come through Auschwitz in order to give up my Jewish heritage.

At the end of the summer, the camp was disbanded and we were distributed
to a number of schools. Jack and I were assigned to a school on the island of
Visingso, on the second largest lake in Sweden, Lake Wattern. Arthur was
sent to a hospital because the doctors thought he had a mild case of tuberculosis; he joined us a year later at a school in Nasviken in northern Sweden. As
students left the country for other parts of the world, the schools were combined and reconstituted and we were moved periodically. At Visingso, the
teenagers in my group—most of whom were about seventeen years old—
were from all parts of Eastern Europe, but mostly from Poland, Romania,
Czechoslovakia, and Hungary. There, we studied at the high school level.
English and Modern Hebrew were the most popular languages and history
and math completed the curriculum.

I was ready to learn and to grow. In particular for me, it was a chance to
grow intellectually. This time was a period of great discovery—a new world
of literature and history. I began to imagine a new world of great possibilities.
Although my new life was happy, in the inner recesses of my being I was still
grief-stricken and furious at the loss of my family. Yet, we behaved as our
parents had raised us, turning our energies toward building new lives.

The teachers were also survivors. One of the outstanding teachers was Elizabeth Mohr from Kecshemet, Hungary, whom we called "Baba," a Hungarian word for doll. She was a very gifted counselor for all of us. She gave us
much needed confidence and encouragement.

The school facilities were like an all-season camp, with one primary building for dining and social events. In addition to regular classes, we organized
a soccer team. Soccer became our passion. Eventually we arranged a match
with a local team. They were much better than we were, but we didn't mind.
Playing soccer was what regular kids did and we were happy to be able to
play. Socials became more and more important. We organized dances on Saturday and Sunday nights and developed romantic relationships. We danced to
recorded music of the great American bands, but Israeli folk dancing was a
continuing favorite.

In general, we kept within school precincts, with no direct social contact
with the local population; I don't know whether that was by design or circumstance. But as a result, we formed warm and close friendships among
ourselves, happy in our newfound freedom. Many of these friendships have
lasted my lifetime. Although some of my friends settled in widespread parts
of the world, we still make the effort and time to see one another. Whenever
we meet is a special occasion, as though we hadn't been separated by time or
distance.

From time to time, prominent guest speakers came to the school to see for
themselves the survivors of a vanished world. One of my favorite visitors was

Cantor Leo Rosenbluth of the Jewish congregation Mosaiska Forsamlingen of Stockholm. He used to come for an overnight stay at the school to give us a recital of Jewish folk songs and lead us in singing. Sometimes he would stay for two or three days. I led the Shabbat morning services at the school and developed a reputation as a fine singer. So when Rosenbluth visited, he had already heard about me and sought me out. Sometimes he would divide the boys into two groups for rounds; he would lead one group and would say, "My colleague Laszlo will lead the other group." He was a man of overpowering presence, so our relationship could not be called a personal friendship, but I was greatly flattered when he called me colleague.

Unknown to me at the time, Rosenbluth had asked the headmaster for permission to take me to Stockholm for serious musical studies; he had made arrangements for me to have a scholarship. The headmaster of the school declined on my behalf without consulting me. The directors of the school were Zionist and were determined that we go to Palestine. The fact that I was free from the Nazis did not yet mean that I was allowed to make independent decisions.

As it turned out, my path would lead me to the United States. I visited Sweden a quarter of a century later and tried to reach Cantor Rosenbluth, but when I was in Stockholm he was on holiday in Switzerland. I left a note asking if he remembered "the Hungarian boy with the good voice." After his return home, he wrote me that indeed he remembered but he also added, "You did well going to the USA."

Most of the kids at the school planned to go to Israel—then Palestine under British control. The state of Israel was only a dream then, since it was not officially born until 1948. However, the British did everything they could to prevent emigration to Palestine. Many survivors tried to enter Palestine illegally but the British Navy patrolled the Mediterranean Sea, stopping the ships and imprisoning the passengers in camps on Cyprus. I later learned that my sister Iren had left Hungary and returned to a displaced persons camp in Germany where she met her future husband, Lali. Together, they crossed the Italian mountains on foot, walking through snow as high as her knees. Iren, pregnant with her first child Shoshana, sailed on an illegal ship toward Palestine. The British Navy stopped her ship and forced it to Cyprus. In 1948, Iren, her husband Lali and her daughter Shoshana, born in Cyprus, finally made it to the new state of Israel. They had two other children, Moshe and Tovah. My sister Iren had ten grandchildren.

I also learned that Ilona, who had stayed in Budapest, met her future husband Laszlo Frank. They settled in his hometown Csokno in northeast Hungary where they had two children Aniko and Shandor. Each of her children had two children themselves who are accomplished in their own right:

Aniko's children are Erika and Anita and Shandor's children are Agnes and Dori.

In 1947, some of my friends began to leave for many parts of the world. Arthur, who had family in New York, was the first to go. Jack, my closest friend, who also had an extended family in New York, was next. In order to receive a visa for the United States, some person or institution had to guarantee that you would not become a public charge, a burden to the country. Since I had no family in the United States, Jack—ever the loyal friend—obtained a full scholarship for me from a small seminary in Williamsburg, Brooklyn. And so, with that important document in hand, I received a student visa to study for four years in the United States. I was eager to move on to a new stage in my life, especially in America.

Chapter Eleven

A New Life

I sailed from Goteborg on the *Drottningholm* on January 3rd, 1948. The Jewish community of Stockholm, the Mosaiska Forsamlingen, had paid for my passage. Several of my fellow students were on board with me: Eli Stern, who later became a builder, and Imre Zwiebel, who became a professor of chemistry. I shared a cabin with a Latvian man I did not know. The ship's accommodations, no doubt economy class, were quite adequate; the food in the dining room was excellent. Crossing the North Atlantic in the winter is an adventure I wouldn't recommend. The ocean was stormy for the greater part of the voyage and I was seasick for several days. My dizziness made a task as simple as getting dressed challenging. However, after I regained my footing, I enjoyed the voyage and looked forward to landing in New York.

When we pulled into New York harbor on January 13th, much of the ship was covered with thick ice. The winter day when I disembarked on New York's West Side was cold and gray, the city's streets covered with dirty snow. I was curious but calm as I took my first steps in the new land. Several of my friends had to spend a few days on Ellis Island before they were admitted to the country but, since I spoke English well enough, I was admitted immediately.

Jack met me at the pier and welcomed me to the new world of the United States. I grabbed my one suitcase and we took the subway to Williamsburg, Brooklyn. A sparsely-furnished rental room above Stone's kosher deli on the corner of Lee Avenue and Roebling Street was my first home in this new world. At Stone's, I discovered delicious American corned beef. In my small room, I woke each night at 2 A.M. to the jarring sound of streetcars coming to a screeching halt.

A new time of testing had begun. I was full of questions. How would I fare alone in this immense city teeming with new immigrants? I missed terribly the warm camaraderie of sharing a house with my schoolmates in Sweden, but that was not the real world. We were too sheltered there. In New York, despite Jack's proximity, I was conscious of being alone and was quite anxious.

Soon after my arrival, I entered the yeshiva, Torah V'Daat—a religious institute for advanced Jewish studies. The institute had a secular high school in the afternoon. Since my primary aim was admission to college, a diploma from an accredited high school was an absolute requirement. Although I had spent two and a half years in a residential school in Sweden, it was not accredited in the States. I pursued my high school diploma with great energy in addition to the afternoon high school of Torah V'Daat. I also attended the Washington Irving High School in Manhattan in the evenings to advance more rapidly toward my goal.

Fortunately, I received sufficient financial support from the New York Association of New Americans, a branch of the United Jewish Appeal. During my first interview there with a young social worker, I informed her of my stay in Sweden at the end of World War II. "Oh," she said, "I see you went to Sweden to be rehabilitated."

I was astonished by her remark because it was so far from the happy human experience that I had known there. I answered, "Rehabilitated? I did not need rehabilitation. I had a wonderful time there. Perhaps much of the world needs rehabilitation."

New York was a great city in 1948 and I enjoyed my time there. I made steady progress in school. Everything was going well until a medical exam produced a diagnosis of presumptive tuberculosis and my forward momentum came to a sudden halt. I was sent to Denver, Colorado, to a sanatorium for observation and treatment. I was admitted in April 1949 and stayed until January 29, 1950, yet, all tests proved negative; I never had TB. Finally, I asked to be discharged and I returned to New York to resume my studies. Although I had lost valuable time, I was more determined than ever to succeed. Within a year and a half, I completed the requirements for high school graduation, took the college entrance exam at Brooklyn College and was admitted in the fall of 1950.

The first time I walked on the campus, the chimes of the library bell tower welcomed me, sounding the hour. I entered a world I had sought since early childhood; to me, Brooklyn College represented prestige and achievement. My dear friend Zoltan Fried, the only friend I made in Auschwitz, entered Brooklyn College at the same time. We moved to Flatbush, closer to school, and shared a furnished room on St. Paul's Place. Zoltan went on to attend the

Massachusetts Institute of Technology and Brandeis University. He was a professor at the University of Massachusetts until his death in 2003.

Completely on my own financially, I worked on weekends, holidays, and summer vacations at a Catskill Mountains resort. This work schedule gave me freedom to attend college on a full-time basis. This kind of employment was not uncommon in those days for young actors and college students who were self-supporting. After two years at Brooklyn College, I dropped out to pursue voice training privately in New York.

I was supposed to return to Sweden after four years, but Congress passed a law that year permitting 100,000 refugees to come to the United States. The law also had a provision allowing people who were here on student visas to apply for a new status, that of immigrant, allowing me to stay permanently and eventually to become a U. S. citizen. President Harry S Truman signed the bill into law in 1948.

Years later, I was able to thank him personally. I met him at an airport in Clarksburg, West Virginia, in the fall of 1962. He had come on a political trip during the congressional elections and I was a student rabbi there for the High Holy Days. My wife, Judy, was flying in from Cincinnati to meet me, and Truman's plane could not take off until the incoming plane landed. Standing outside the small terminal, he was surrounded by local politicians. I very badly wanted to greet him, so I walked past the group several times. Finally one of the group asked, "Do you want to say hello to the President?" After some hesitation, I approached him. When I thanked him for signing the bill, he said, "I'm glad you stayed."

Although it was my ambition to attend college and study economics, my limited knowledge of English was not sufficient for college-level work at that time. A little more seasoning was necessary. The consequence of leaving college, though, was being drafted into the U. S. Army in 1954.

I took basic training at Fort Dix, New Jersey, and advanced armor training at Fort Knox, Kentucky. Being in the U. S. Army enabled me to experience American life in a completely different way, living in close quarters with young men from all regions of the country. This experience had a lasting impact on my understanding of the country and contributed greatly to my ability to truly become an American and feel at home in my new country.

Upon completion of training at Fort Knox, my entire company was assigned to Germany, except for one GI of Polish origin and me. The time was the height of the Cold War and we both had relatives behind the Iron Curtain. I suspect it was a matter of security that we were both sent to Scofield Barracks in Honolulu, Hawaii, home of the famous movie, *From Here to Eternity*. I was very proud that fewer than ten years after my liberation from a concentration camp by the 82nd Airborne Division, I was a Private First Class in a tank company of the 27th Infantry Regiment of the 25th Infantry Division of the U.S. Army.

My military service in Hawaii would mark a pivotal point in my life. Only a few months after arriving there, with the approach of the Jewish High Holy Days, I met Chaplain Samuel Sobel, Commander, U. S. Navy, and volunteered to assist him in religious worship. He asked me, "What can you do?"

"I know all the music," I said. He asked me to sing a prayer and I did. The impact was immediate. I became his Chaplain's Assistant and was soon transferred to Division Headquarters. Thus, I was discovered in the middle of the Pacific in a Quonset hut that served as a chapel in Pearl Harbor. I was recognized as a gifted young man, not just a displaced person or a faceless immigrant, and I was grateful for that.

In Chaplain Sobel, I found a mentor and friend who cared deeply about people. As Chaplain, he was loved and respected by soldiers, sailors and airmen of all ranks. He was totally devoted to his chaplaincy. His wife Shirley made me feel like a member of their family.

My work as Chaplain's Assistant brought many strands of my being into focus. Above all, I enjoyed relating to our military congregants in a religious context. Many passionate conversations with Chaplain Sobel about social issues led him to raise the idea of the rabbinate with me. He was a graduate of the Reform Movement's Jewish Institute of Religion in New York, a liberal seminary. He encouraged me to consider becoming a rabbi when I completed my time in the Army. It was not a totally new idea to me. My parents had often thought about it and mentioned it to me. But entering the Hebrew Union College's Jewish Institute of Religion required a Bachelor of Arts degree. I still needed two more years of undergraduate study.

To paraphrase the great American playwright Tennessee Williams, the kindness of strangers has repeatedly played an important role at key points in my life: a person appears on the scene at a critical juncture, performs a significant function, and moves on. Such a person was Frank L. Weill, Chairman of the Board of Hebrew Union College. Upon Chaplain Sobel's suggestion, Mr. Weill recommended to the College that I be admitted. When I arrived in Cincinnati, I discovered that Mr. Weill had also provided a full scholarship for me. I am deeply indebted to him for his generosity and kindness. Simultaneously, I entered the University of Cincinnati to continue work toward a B.A. degree in sociology.

Settled at the Hebrew Union College, I hit the books at full speed. With the scholarship and the GI Bill of Rights benefits, I was free to focus all my energy on my studies. After several detours on a very complex road, I was at last in the right place and everything came together for me. I received the B.A. degree in sociology from the University of Cincinnati and then a Master's Degree with Honors from the Hebrew Union College. I am forever grateful to the Hebrew Union College for opening its doors to me. I received rabbinic ordination in Cincinnati in June 1963, marking the fulfillment of an almost impossible dream.

My personal life changed dramatically during my student years in Cincinnati. In 1960, I met a wonderful girl, Judith Ann Mitman, a second generation Cincinnatian. It was clear to both of us that we were meant for each other. A year later, we were married in the Chapel of the Hebrew Union College. Our marriage of unconditional love was very special and we were blessed with two beautiful daughters, Julie and Deborah, and five grandchildren, Zoe, Hannah, Samuel, Naomi, and Yael. Our sons-in-law, Peter and Alan, complete our family circle.

By this time, Arthur had settled on Long Island and had become a successful garment designer. Jack, whose ambition had been to become a playwright, settled in Spain. Sam Gluck, my childhood friend from Derecske who first confirmed the truth about the crematoria, moved to Stamford, Connecticut and became a chef. Eli Stern, who had traveled with me from Sweden and was my roommate in Williamsburg, became a successful builder in New York State. Chaim Yisroael Perl, one of my classmates in Sweden, became a teacher and writer in Ramat Gan, Israel. Henry Friedman, another classmate from Sweden, moved to Canada and became a land developer. My friends have accomplished much and I rejoice in their achievements.

Soon after ordination, a committee from a newly-formed congregation Temple Rodef Shalom in Falls Church, Virginia, arrived at Hebrew Union College to interview candidates for the pulpit. The committee met with several newly ordained rabbis and selected me by a unanimous vote. The fact that I was older than my classmates worked in my favor. I was delighted to take up my post on July 1st, 1963 in the national Capital area with its strong cultural institutions.

The congregation, Temple Rodef Shalom (Pursuer of Peace), had a small but enthusiastic group of about sixty families and drew its membership from Falls Church, Arlington, and Fairfax Counties. Our members were highly educated people, many of them serving in important posts in the Federal Civil Service, with great expectations of congregational life: intellectual freedom, passionate commitment to social justice, and a genuine spiritual quest.

The congregation and I wanted to create a community with a nurturing spirit—welcoming by its very nature, a place people would want to come to, a community they would want to be part of. We were long on ideas but short on experience and it took time to find our bearings. I was young, full of energy and hope that we would be successful. While the congregation did not yet have a home to pray in or even a piece of land, we had a set of prayer books, a pulpit Bible, a pair of silver Shabbat candlesticks, a Kiddush cup, a Torah, and me. We worshiped in churches, rented public school space for religious school and met in private homes for lectures. High Holy Day services were held in the sanctuary of a neighboring church. I was pleased to be able to act as cantor as well as rabbi, and from the beginning first-rate music was an important part of our services.

I didn't mind building from scratch; I thrived on it. I had seen so much destruction in Europe that working to create something where nothing had been before was both exciting and rewarding. I looked forward to the future, building a new life, a new community, and putting a new name on the religious map.

With devoted leadership in the congregation, Rodef Shalom grew stage by stage. Its growth paralleled the growth both of the nation's Capital and the Jewish component of its population. Before World War II, there had been only one Reform congregation in Northern Virginia, the historic Temple Beth El in Alexandria, founded in 1859 and, for years, it struggled to maintain its membership. The decade of the 1950s brought a tremendous influx of young professional families to Washington, mostly employed in the burgeoning agencies of the federal government. The good schools and affordable housing in the area drew many of those families to its neighborhoods.

Expansion and accommodation pains at Temple Beth El produced a congregational split, the breakaway families formed Temple Rodef Shalom in 1962. When the congregation was a scant two years old, a search was begun for a permanent home. Land was acquired in 1964, and in September 1970 we moved into a brand-new, beautiful building just in time for the High Holy Days. The following year, we opened a pre-school in addition to our religious school and, within three years, the pre-school was full. Our religious school flourished as well. In time, our young people came to consider the congregation as an extension of their homes. Our building has been enlarged, and enlarged again, to accommodate a growing population and the needs of the religious school, library, and offices. Today, Rodef Shalom is one of the outstanding congregations of metropolitan Washington and is the largest Jewish congregation in the Commonwealth of Virginia, reaching nearly 1,400 families in 2007.

Rodef Shalom developed its core identity during the sixties, a revolutionary period in American life. The nation was challenged on every front to live up to the highest ideals of the American ethos—the war in Vietnam, unrest on college campuses, and the heroic struggle for civil rights were the soul-searing issues of the time. As a concentration camp survivor, human rights issues are very important to me.

Fairfax County, Virginia—Rodef Shalom's home—is a prosperous, fast-growing, dynamic community, but it contains pockets of poverty and homelessness. The Temple joined with like-minded people to help fund shelter for transient individuals. We have a soup kitchen run by volunteers who prepare and deliver food to the needy, often senior citizens living alone. On Christmas Day, hundreds of our members prepare and deliver complete dinners for 300 people in shelters.

In the fall of 1979, the attention of the congregation was focused on the plight of the thousands of refugees seeking to escape from Southeast Asia after the collapse of South Vietnam. Their sufferings evoked in our congregation the memory of the plight of Jews before and during the Second World War. With the help of the Hebrew Immigration Aid Society, congregation members sponsored five Vietnamese families, bringing them to Falls Church, finding them homes and work, and collecting donations of money, furniture, clothing and household appliances to help them settle. The resettlement efforts were successful enough that later the Hebrew Immigration Aid Society sought the Temple's help in sponsoring a Hungarian and then a Romanian Jewish family.

All these efforts to build community are a reflection of our synagogue's religious ideals. We not only pray for the well-being of our community, we roll up our sleeves and work for it. My work affirms my faith that Judaism has something very important to impart to our congregants—that it can uplift the human spirit and help it reach great heights through worship, study, and a commitment to the common good.

Staying in one congregation in one community through a career is exceptional for a rabbi. This longevity has been especially rewarding for me because I have been able to watch the generations in motion. It has been a privilege to touch individual lives as they grow—as children, as teenagers, as young parents, and eventually as grandparents. Coping with loss, whether timely or untimely, is an important part of being in the congregation. As individuals and as a community, we rally to the side of the individual and the family, so that no one feels alone. This is an essential part of our religious tradition, and very helpful at a difficult time in a person's life.

In addition to the activities of our temple, I personally became very involved in a range of issues in my community. I testified at hearings in Arlington and Fairfax Counties on behalf of fair housing; efforts to combat deeply held racial prejudice in our community eventually led to integration. I became involved with the Fairfax County Community Action Project to combat poverty. I served on the board of the Falls Church Cerebral Palsy Center, which provides much-needed care for children and their families. One of my most satisfying experiences was serving on the founding board of the Hospice of Northern Virginia; today, it is one of the most successful of its kind in the nation, providing compassionate care at the end of life for both patients and their families. Finally, I am a great supporter of the public school system, where children from all walks of life can learn and grow together and I was proud to have had the opportunity to serve on the Fairfax County Superintendent's Advisory Committee and on its Human Rights Committee. I was also appointed by Virginia's Governor Douglas Wilder to serve as a member on the Council on Human Rights.

Often in congregational life, a rabbi moves from sorrow to joy in a single day. Being fully present at each kind of event is a profoundly bonding experience. Being a rabbi in a contemporary American Reform Jewish congregation calls upon the entirety of the rabbi's resources as a person, preacher, teacher, pastor, friend, and counselor. No one has all the qualities needed, but, if you are fortunate, you may grow in time so that your strengths are valued and your weaknesses overlooked or forgiven. My personal experience with one of the most devastating times and places in human history helped me learn how to help people in times of both crisis and joy. Having survived all that I survived, I believe I learned how to walk into a range of profoundly human situations, joyful and sad, and feel that I can be of assistance. I am grateful to all who encouraged me to go from strength to strength and stayed with me to bring in the harvest.

I have been back to Hungary many times. The first trip was when my children were quite young, in the early '80s. I felt a natural pull from my birthplace. I was curious about what Derecske looked like and how I would feel being back. I needed to close that chapter of my life.

When I arrived, some forty years after I had left, I discovered that the landscape and the general physical nature of the village was largely the same. Childhood memories flooded over me. What excitement to feel the earth shaking as the train roared into our town's station, the station that always held great magic for me. To see once again the small waiting room filled with pipe smoke. I was shocked that everything was so much smaller than I remembered it: in a minute and a half by car we were through the entire town. Many of the houses had been torn down and new ones built, but the church is the same, as is the City Hall. Derecske was and wasn't the same.

I visited the Jewish cemetery. It was the only part of town that was Jewish. Nothing else Jewish remained in the town. Standing there, I felt solitary and almost abandoned. The weeds were tall; the stones had fallen over. It was important for me to stand there as an adult and see the tombstones of family, friends and neighbors and remember all that had been. My grandmother's grave is the only one of my family there. She died when I was a little boy.

Several years ago in 2003, I visited Warsaw, Krakow, Budapest and Prague. One of the reasons I decided to finish this book were the empty synagogues I saw in all these cities. Synagogues that were once vibrant and alive with prayer and song and worship, silent. Buildings were there but not people. Those empty buildings compelled me to find my voice and tell my story.

On the same trip, I went back to Auschwitz.

I had always wanted to go back and stand on the train platform that changed my life forever. I wondered what I would feel. Fear? Anger? I had images in my mind about what it looked like but I wanted to see how reality compared to my memories. I wanted to walk across to the other side, like those who took their last walk. I wanted to find the place where the barrack I had slept in had stood.

Yet, the place I visited was not Auschwitz-Birkenau, but simply the place where Auschwitz-Birkenau had been. It was like a bare stage, the props and scenery gone: denuded of meaning. For me, the remains of the camp – the ruins of the crematoria, the broken pieces of concrete of the gas chamber – had no meaning for me. They deny the true character, the true existence, of Auschwitz-Birkenau. Without the Nazis themselves, the terror and fear of the place was gone. Unless you had been there, you would never know the true barbarity, the true nature of this hell on earth.

History can vanish. No one who goes to visit Auschwitz-Birkenau will ever know what it meant to be held prisoner there by the Nazis. The essence of the place has disappeared except in the minds of those who experienced it first-hand. I am grateful to Elie Wiesel, Primo Levi, and the many, many others who have written about their experience—so it will not be forgotten.

While there, I saw a group of Israeli soldiers who had been brought to Auschwitz as part of their training. Israel, a thriving, strong Jewish homeland, was unimaginable to me in 1944. Seeing those Israeli army officers walk through what was left of Auschwitz-Birkenau was surreal. Some of the Israeli soldiers, children of Holocaust survivors, spoke in Hungarian to me. To watch the children of Hungarian Jews, survivors of the Holocaust, native Israelis visiting the place where their grandparents had been put to death, where their parents had survived, was an unbelievable experience. Who could have forseen that?

It has been quite a journey, from childhood in a pastoral village in Hungary to the fiery hell of Auschwitz-Birkenau as a teenager, to newfound freedom on the banks of the Potomac, and lifelong service to one congregation, building a new community.

Above all, after a precious love shared with Judy for 39 years until her untimely death in 2000 and after raising two beautiful human beings, Julie and

Deborah, I now proudly and happily wear the hat of "Grandpa" to Zoe, Sam, Hannah, Naomi and Yael.

The most satisfying volunteer work I have done over the years has been speaking to high school students about my experience as a teenager in the Nazi concentration camps. The students are amazing: they are deeply moved by having a living survivor share his story with them. Hearing the truth from a survivor who was close to their age at the time of his suffering makes a profound impact on them. Their thoughtful questions indicate a deep humanity that is gratifying to me. Perhaps, for the first time in their young lives, they understand the destructive power of religious bigotry and racial prejudice.

When I talk with these students, I am often asked, *Rabbi, after Auschwitz-Birkenau, do you have faith in God?*

I have struggled over the years to answer that question.

The Holocaust represents the shattering of all ethical boundaries by the Nazi Nation State. The event challenges culture and faith. How can we talk about God after the Holocaust?

Established notions about divine omnipotence raise significant questions: *How could God allow it? Where was God's providence, God's love?* In spite of Auschwitz-Birkenau, I can't let go of God. Or, more precisely, I seek to understand God in a new context. This search is not only for these young people but for myself as well.

My search took me to man's first contact with God in the book of Genesis 2:19 & 20:

> And the Lord God formed out of the earth all the wild beasts and all the birds of the sky, and brought them to the man to see what he would call them; and whatever the man called each living creature, that would be its name. And the man gave names to all the cattle and to the birds of the sky and to all the wild beasts, but for Adam no fitting helper was found.

Why didn't God name these creatures Himself? Why did He give this task to the first human being? Couldn't the Creator of the cosmos name every creature? How could the first human name the creatures—*define them*—unless God had already endowed him with the ability to do so? The ability to think. The human mind. The mind explores, discovers, defines nature itself. The gathering of knowledge is a God-given gift. To what end this knowledge is applied, for good or ill, is a matter of choice.

Does man have freedom to choose? Maimonides, a twelfth century Jewish philosopher, author of *The Mishneh Torah*, and one of the great authorities of the Jewish tradition, affirms that:

Free will is given to every human being. If we wish to incline ourselves toward goodness and righteousness, we are free to do so; and if we wish to incline ourselves toward evil, we are also free to do that. From Scripture (Genesis 3:22) we learn that the human species, with its knowledge of good and evil, is unique among all the earth's creatures. Of our own accord, by our own faculty of intelligence and understanding, we can distinguish between good and evil, doing as we choose. Nothing holds us back from making this choice between good and evil—the power is in our hands. (As translated in the *Gates of Repentance*, p. 7)

These two God-given instruments, the mind and free will, help me to understand how Auschwitz came to be. Through these two gifts, God formed a partnership with men and women that will shape the destiny of humankind. The accumulation of knowledge gave every individual enormous power for good or for ill. Having free will, we can choose to use this power for good or ill. Our choices are our own. That fact is inescapable. And scary.

And yet—my hope is that women and men will choose the good. Imagine what could be accomplished if we accepted that the choices are our own. That each and every human being is accountable. Responsible.

The students ask, *Do you still have faith in God?* And I ask them, *Does God have faith in us that we will use the gifts of mind and free will and choose well?* If each and every one of us were to choose a moral course, we may yet repair the broken fragments of our world and vindicate God's faith in us.

References

Baganz, Carina. *Ten Weeks Concentration Camp Wobbelin: A Camp in Mecklenburg/ Germany in 1945*, Published by Forderverein Mahn—und Gedenkstatten Wobbelin e. V. in cooperation with Landeszentrale fur politsche Bildung Mecklenburg-Vorpommern, 2005.

Braham, Randolph L. *The Politics of Genocide. The Holocaust in Hungary, Volume I* New York, The Rosenthal Institute for Holocaust Studies and Columbia University, 1994.

Gilbert, Martin. *The Holocaust*, New York, Holt, Rinehart and Winston, 1985.

——, *Never Again: a History of the Holocaust*, New York, Universe, 2000.

Hilberg, Raul. *The Destruction of the European Jews*, Volume Two, New York, Holmes and Meier, 1985.

Kenny, Robert W. *Temple Rodef Shalom: the First Twenty-five Years*, McLean, Virginia, Associations International, 1988.

Levy, Primo. *Survival in Auschwitz, Reawakening*.

Liedke, Karl. "Destruction Through Work: Lodz Jews in the Bussing Truck Factory in Braunschweig, 1944–1945," Jerusalem, *Yad Vashem Studies, XXX*, 2002, pp. 153–187.

Linton, Leonard. *Military Government by the 82nd Airborne*.

Peter, Ujvari. *Zsido Lexicon*, Budapest, Zsido Lexicon, 1929.

Sachs, Neily. *O'The Chimneys*, Farrar, Strauss and Giroux, New York, 1969.

Schwartzbart, Andre. *The Last of the Just*, New York, Atheneum Publishers, 1961.

Swiebocki, Henryk. *Auschwitz 1940–1945, Volume IV, The Resistance Movement*, Auschwitz-Birkenau State Museum, Oswiecim (Auschwitz), Poland, 2000.

Wiesel, Eli. *Night*, Avon Books, New York, 1969.

The Gates of Repentance.